Book Reviews for Ult
A Holistic Guide for Strength and Balance
Changing Times

Ultimate Self Care is a must read for everyone. We are living in interesting times, where there are new devices, new stresses, and new illnesses, showing up every day on the planet. HOW do we navigate this? This book is an excellent guide, resource, and companion on your journey. You will learn WHY you may be experiencing what you are going through AND you will be taken through very practical techniques and tools that you can do from home now. This book is incredibly put together with love, dedication, and a genuine caring for your own personal journey. The *Ultimate Self Care* book is incredibly thorough and gives you more than just information. You will get tools, follow up websites, and get in depth information to take you further. I highly recommend this book. At work places, pick up this book and form groups within that workplace. Imagine what could happen? If you start this book, you will never look back. Welcome to the first day of a new journey of transformation for YOU.

- Dr. Divi Chandna, M.D., Intuitive Coach
  Mind Body Spirit Center
  www.drdivi.com

The *Ultimate Self Care* is a self-help book and I love it. This book should be read by everyone. I don't think anyone could read it and not find something that resonates with them. It is the kind of book that you want to read again and start implementing some of the exercises. The author authentically shares her life experiences and philosophy. There is a great need for self-care, simply because our day to day life contains so much that is out of balance. Many of us suffer the stressors from work, family, and obligations, which rob us of our vitality. This book is a practical guide that starts with where you are. It asks you to take responsibility for implementing a strategy of self-care. The book is very well-written and smartly organized. It is a rare book amongst a growing pool of 'spiritual' or 'new-age' publications, which offers very practical guidance to people who are navigating their spiritual journey. Compassionately, Barbara takes the reader step-by-step through every aspect of the deeper understanding of oneself. Her style is simple, flawless, effortless, and very well researched. It resonates with her own heart felt and true experiences. I wish all work places could change their outlook and create balance by following the author's suggestion. The book is an overall winner to bring balance between work and relationship, with one's own self.

- Bhavna Solecki
  Founder/Director
  Inner Evolution Center Ltd.
  Holistic Center for Pain and Stress Management.
  Vancouver, BC, Canada

Like the very definition of the term 'ultimate' (incapable of further analysis; final; definitive), Barbara's book *Ultimate Self-Care* is just that – absolutely definitive, comprehensive, and all encompassing. It ranges in scope from a metaphysical, theological, and cosmic perspective on self-care, in relation to the core of our beloved planet, to the most practical pointers on how to practice self-care for oneself and others. Barbara is speaking about this topic from many levels: as a skilled counselor and social worker, a holistic practitioner, a spiritual visionary, and finally, as a human being, able to empathize with all manner of human experience. She has birthed this book from the very depths of her being and the result is truly awesome.

Barbara's emphasis on the need for active and creative self-care is certainly in agreement with the premise of many doctors who integrate traditional and alternative medicine. So, Bernie Segal, in his book *Magic, Medicine, and Miracles,* spoke of working with exceptional cancer patients who were always active in their recovery, never merely passively surrendering to medical authority.

Deepak Chopra, in his latest book, co-authored with R. Tanzi, speaks of the need for a healing lifestyle on every level, to counter the possible onset of any major disease. Barbara's book truly awakens this capacity for creative self-care and active recovery in anyone reading this book and following its precepts.

Dealing with constant stress and burnout is very much like being lost in a labyrinth. This book helps to provide the sacred thread that will lead us out of this impasse. For anyone interested in self-care from any perspective, look no further. The answers have been given. What an extraordinary service Barbara has rendered.

- Dr. Shirley Anne McMurtry, Ph.D.
  Vancouver, BC, Canada

It reads well, is researched carefully, and covers a wide spectrum of spiritualties, philosophies, and psychology. When you interject your own experience, you bring the suggestions and ideas closer to the reader, the goals become more attainable. Congratulations for a work well done, instructive, and useful. Many, many thanks.

- Grazia Merler, Trento, Italy

Barbara Halcrow, MSW, began her career as a social worker, trainer, and healer. On this path, Barbara worked in diverse urban and rural communities across Canada in the areas of child protection, domestic violence, sexual abuse, mental health & addictions, individual & family counseling, and adult/older adult healthcare. While in healthcare, she held numerous leadership roles across the healthcare continuum in acute, rehabilitation, and community sectors.

Barbara Halcrow has always had a strong connection to the beauty and power of nature, the realm of spirit, and the energy of love that flows through life. Over the years, this inner connection has led to further spiritual development and energy studies at home and abroad. In 2011, Barbara Halcrow self-published her first book, a partial memoir entitled, *"Spiritual Intelligence, How Your Spirit will Lead You to Health, Happiness and Success"*.

Barbara believes that by offering ourselves more conscious self-nourishment and by embracing the healing power of gratitude, compassion, and forgiveness for ourselves and others, we also enhance our own ability to create swifter, positive changes in our lives – and in turn, positively affect the lives of others.

Dedication

This writing is dedicated to anyone who feels the need for more self-nourishment – especially to those who give so much of themselves caring for others in their daily work or in their personal lives.

Barbara Halcrow

ULTIMATE SELF-CARE

A Holistic Guide for Strength and Balance in Changing Times

AUSTIN MACAULEY PUBLISHERS™

LONDON • CAMBRIDGE • NEW YORK • SHARJAH

Ordering Information:
Quantity sales: special discounts are available on quantity purchases by corporations, associations, and others. For details, contact the publisher at the address below.

Publisher's Cataloguing-in-Publication data
Halcrow, Barbara.
Ultimate Self-Care, A Holistic Guide for Strength and Balance in Changing Times

ISBN 9781641820899 (Paperback)
ISBN 9781641820912 (Hardback)
ISBN 9781641820905 (E-Book)

The main category of the book — Self-Help / Motivational & Inspirational

www.austinmacauley.com

First Published (2018)
Austin Macauley Publishers Ltd ™
40 Wall Street, 28th Floor
New York, NY 10005
USA
mail-usa@austinmacauley.com
+1 (646) 5125767

Acknowledgments

I would not have written this book without my involvement and deep caring for the people I have worked with as colleagues and clients over the years in two Canadian provinces, the Yukon Territory, and Seoul, Korea.

In particular, I would like to offer my gratitude to the knowledgeable and skilled women and men in their roles as colleagues, managers and directors throughout Vancouver Coastal Health – a progressive organization in British Columbia that's offered meaningful opportunities for me to give service to others and to learn and grow in invaluable ways.

I also thank my spirited and encouraging family members, especially my sisters, Catherine Halcrow and Lindsay Barber.

Much appreciation as well to some special friends, Gisela Good, Brenda Whitehall, Carole Britton, Dr. Anne McMurtry, Anett Manering, and Audrey Clements for their insightful and consistent support.

Additionally, I want to give acknowledgement to Brigitte Petersen for her helpful, preliminary editing.

To Doug Volz, one of my favorite piano players – thank you for giving me the gift of your soul's beautiful music that I continue to listen to for compassionate heart openings.

Finally, my deepest gratitude is to the eternal, guiding, and transformative energy of love that lies within each of us and gently nudges us to trust in the voice of our own hearts.

Introduction

Are you feeling tired and stressed with little time to care for yourself? Is your business or workplace going through continuous changes that leave you wondering if there will be any downtime? Are you in the people-helping field or a caregiver to anyone, including a family member? Do you want to know if you can make more effective changes to improve some of your current self-care practices?

With so many changes and challenges underway, it is not surprising many of us are more distracted and fatigued from trying to care adequately for our own needs.

We are in a most remarkable, changing, and uncertain time in Earth's history, with significant changes occurring across every segment of global society. Some changes are positive in adding technological convenience and increased wellness to our lives, while other changes are creating the opposite through fear, losses, trauma, and hardship.

While there may be new job creations in some areas, there are also sudden losses due to fiscal restraints, cutbacks, and job obsoletion due to rising automation. There can also be added changes in our own health and then, the health of our family members, resulting in more of us adopting the role of caregiver to our elderly loved ones.

There are also national and international shifts across the global economic and socio-geo-political landscape that are giving rise to significant systemic changes affecting all of humanity. Add in the increasing magnitude and destructiveness of Earth's climate changes to all of the ongoing global transitions, and we have an unprecedented time on this planet, a time where our levels of concern, anxiety, and stresses are increased. The overall immensity of these global shifts potentially affects how we perceive ourselves going forward with future plans and also how we are currently able to attend to our own self-care needs.

Focusing on our need for self-care is a loving and respectful thing to do. Giving proper nourishment to ourselves as we are able to, increases our vitality, self-esteem, and self-confidence. It also allows us to give to others we care about from a more energetic and balanced perspective because we ultimately make better decisions about how much we can give. When we are better nourished, we can hear our own inner guiding voice more clearly.

Within my own life, I had many early challenges to overcome beginning at an early age. In part, because of my strong connection to the nourishment found in nature and from being spiritually guided to find the help and direction I needed, I was able to move through those challenges towards greater healing. It was from the grace and wisdom acquired from those difficult, yet transformative experiences that I decided to write my first book, *Spiritual Intelligence, How Your Spirit Will Lead You to Health, Happiness and Success* (2011). All of our life experiences have meaning and purpose.

ULTIMATE SELF-CARE, A Holistic Guide for Strength and Balance in Changing Times, is a unique kind of holistic guidebook that has combined many areas of personal and professional experience and study. For over 30 years, I have practiced as a counsellor, energy healer, social worker, and have held leadership roles across the continuum of health care. These areas include working with people challenged by addictions, mental health issues, abuse, physical disabilities, and many kinds of traumatic life losses through our evolving life transitions. In all of these experiences, I have remained aware of how the energy or spiritual essence of each of us is interconnected with our physical, mind, and emotional selves. Therefore, the focus in this writing has also included this recognition of our human need to address our spiritual needs, whatever that may mean to each of us.

During my career in social work and teaching, I have always tried to be vigilant about my own health. I have also been concerned about the health and wellness of clients, colleagues, friends, and family. In this regard, I have personally experienced the struggle as many of us have, to care for ourselves in practical, balanced ways – ways that take into account the challenges of our work and our need to continue to embrace many advancing changes while we also deal with the range of our personal life experiences, the joys as well as sudden losses and other stresses that we find in our journeys.

We are in an age of awakening – an age of re-discovering what our ancient ancestors knew – that we are human beings of moving energy rather than just matter and as such, we are actually capable of doing more for ourselves in shaping our lives.

ULTIMATE SELF-CARE, *A Holistic Guide for Strength and Balance in Changing Times* encourages a more holistic approach in the fullness of our humanness in how we can change our lives for the better when we place greater emphasis on our own self-care. This emphasis is not about becoming "selfish or self-serving", it is about appreciating all aspects of what we truly need to create wellness, strength, and balance in our lives. We can support ourselves more holistically when we understand how to work with all of our energy systems.

When we know more about our own body's intelligent systems, we can strengthen ourselves by clearing, raising, and protecting our energy. We can become more aware in recognizing situations that have the potential to adversely lower our energy and in doing so, we take preventative steps to maintain our balance and help avoid ill health.

As we care for ourselves and become more fine-tuned with the full range of our natural spiritual senses, we also evolve our appreciation of how we are beautifully holistically constructed and sacredly interwoven in our connection to all of life that surrounds us.

This guidebook looks at many areas of self-care as we attend to our daily routines, at home or at work. Self-care can be a series of small steps – steps that can be managed even in high stress situations – and each step or activity that feels right and doable, becomes important in moving towards our strengthening.

The various sections I address throughout this book are each books unto themselves. My intention is that in your reading, you will feel inspired to explore more of what most captures your interest and assists you to explore it even further.

There is so much information that is coming forward and changing daily that this book's approach and purpose as a "guidebook" will work well. For as much as I have benefitted in my own health by writing this guidebook, I sincerely believe you will also benefit by using its many practical suggestions in the exercises, strategies, and resource links provided.

This book will provide you with information on:

- Understanding your body's intelligent ways of managing energy
- What vibrational medicine is and how it helps us
- What it means to be an empath and how to support yourself
- Using easy ways to clear, raise, and protect your energy at home and at work
- How to have a positive impact on your body's functioning by communicating directly with it and receiving its information
- Breathing and meditation exercises made easy and effective
- Understanding the factors and symptoms that lead to Change Fatigue, Compassion Fatigue and Vicarious Trauma and what you and your worksite can do about it
- Setting better boundaries for self-assertion and clearer communication
- Why we naturally "default to the negative" and how it affects our communication
- Factors that build strength and resiliency
- Importance of energy alive nutrition, adequate sleep, pure water, and routine exercise
- How and what colors influence your energy levels
- How to tune into your heart's own intelligent brain
- How embracing compassion, acceptance, and forgiveness increases your energy and brings you inner peace
- How to more effectively co-create, affirm, and manifest a life that is more aligned with your deeper wishes
- How your improved self-care practices positively affect everyone around you – as well as the health of Earth

Each of us is meant to be here during this remarkable time of change in ours' and Earth's history. The importance of truly knowing who we are as holistic beings and what we are capable of doing to improve the health of our lives and of this planet cannot be understated, – for we are at our own crossroads to make important choices – choices that will ripple across and touch many other souls on their paths.

Even in increasingly challenging circumstances that bring us uncertainty, losses, and confusion, we can still stay balanced, healthy, and resilient. We can do this by choosing to open to the deeper knowledge that lies within us and is being made available to us. We can practice nourishing ourselves with more loving kindness, compassion, and appreciation, the same kind of kindness and tender nourishment that many of us offer to others in our lives.

My hope is that this book will provide supportive reminders, practical information, and other forms of guidance that encourage your self-care in whatever way feels right for you.

Table of Contents

Chapter 1
The Energy That We Are

"If you want to find the secrets of the universe, think in terms of energy, frequency, and vibration."
- Nikola Tesla

We are far more than what we appear to be. Physically, mentally, emotionally, and spiritually, we are an energy system that is intelligent and interconnected with all of nature. Every cell contains the pattern of our existence.

This is not new information, but according to MacLean (2006), author of *The Vibrational Universe*, not until recently with the advancement of technology did our scientific community fully embrace what ancient cultures have known about our relationship with the cosmos – that everything within us and connected to us on this planet and throughout the universe is composed of vibrating atoms and, as such, is eternally in motion.

Obviously, we cannot see this energy vibrating with the naked eye, but we can feel it and often sense it. Even seemingly lifeless objects like rocks vibrate at such a low level we might erroneously assume they are dead and have no energetic life force. We now know this is not the case.

We also witness material breakdowns, decay, and changes in the material world constantly transpiring around us, as all earth forms energetically shift and transform or transmute in the reappearing processes of life and death. We have greater understanding of energetic changes from the physics that tells us energy is never created or destroyed, it can only be changed or transmuted to another form, according to Moskowitz (2014).

This scientific information is powerful in terms of its overall implications. One can say it implies that as a physical energy form, we are also transmutable and infinite. Although our physical body will die in terms of the energetic chemical and electrical systems that shut down and decay, life's ongoing inquiry and debate of the existence and after-life of the energy of human consciousness, soul, or spirit remains.

Have We Lived Before?

There is accumulating evidence through accounts of individuals' other worldly experiences that may guide us towards the human soul as being a conscious energy that endures beyond our earthbound existence. Dr. Wayne Dyer and Dee Garnes' (2015) publication, *Memories of Heaven, Children's Astounding Recollections of the Time Before They Came to Earth*, is a compelling read of countless children's unsolicited stories of their past-life experiences.

These stories are now found to be more universal in nature as children give specific reasons as to why they decided to choose their particular parents – and in so doing also provide astounding details they couldn't possibly know, about their parents' lives before the children were born.

Another book, by Dr. Jim B. Tucker and Dr. Ian Stevenson, (2008), *Life Before Life: A Scientific Investigation of Children's Memories of Previous Lives,* is scientifically researched and offers a fascinating read of children's detailed memories recalling their previous lives including precise locations where they lived, how they died, and information about their family members and their livelihoods. Upon investigation, these reports were found verifiable.

There is also more available documentation of adults who have gone through near-death experiences. Through those spiritual journeys, they have returned to provide us with profound life-altering stories. One extraordinary and medically verified report is from Dr. George G. Ritchie, author of *Return from Tomorrow (2007)* and *My Life After Dying* (1991), who was pronounced dead for nine minutes and returned with life-changing information of his journey.

Not only did he travel around the medical room to view his own deceased body, but he also consciously spiritually transferred himself to another part of the country. Lastly, he travelled to another dimension where he received information from those in spirit form before finally re-entering his body.

"You are not a drop in the ocean. You are the entire ocean in a drop."

– Rumi

Many researchers in varying fields continue to investigate the nature of our energetic existence. One such organization looking at multiple levels of inquiry is the Institute of Noetic Sciences (IONS), founded in 1973 by Apollo 14 astronaut Edgar Mitchell, ScD.

When Dr. Mitchell returned from space after a life-altering event, he proceeded to establish IONS to investigate and advance the understanding of the spectrum of his experience. The institute uses tools and techniques from all existing sciences that involve: neuroscience, psychophysiology, cognitive and personality psychology, computer engineering, the realm of physics to comprehensively study the nature of intuition, consciousness, distant healing, mind matter interactions, and individuals' transformative experiences. (www.noetic.org).

As he travelled back to earth, Dr. Mitchell's powerful epiphany left him transformed about the nature of human consciousness in connection to the universe around him. He later relayed the following statement of this event in an interview with Dr. Barbara McNeil, his colleague at the IONS:

"My understanding of the distinct separateness and relative independence of movement of those cosmic bodies was shattered. I was overwhelmed with the sensation of physically and mentally extending out into the cosmos. The restraints and boundaries of flesh and bone fell away."

He went on to describe that this same experience was more like a "savikalpa samadhi" moment – a moment whereby "an individual recognizes the separateness of all things, yet

23

understands that the separateness is but an illusion" (McNeil, 2006, pp. 8-9).

From Dr. Mitchell's impetus and the many researchers that signed on in the past years, the IONS's extensive explorations concerning the nature and expansiveness of human consciousness and how it interacts with the world are notable and offered globally in distinguished academic scientific publications.

The Body's Energy Systems

Looking more closely at the human energetic construct we can say that our body has its own intelligent and complex energy systems that work collaboratively and synergistically to create optimum functioning and health. One of the best things we can do to support our overall health is understand the areas of ourselves that we normally do not physically see, but we can definitely experience to varying degrees.

As vibrational beings, we continuously shift and expand our energy in conjunction with our sense of wellness. Our overall energy is influenced by our thoughts, attitudes, beliefs, and feelings, and they in turn come full circle to impact our physical health. These interwoven energy systems create an electro-magnetic charge that naturally extends outward and can be experienced by people, animals, and plants. All living matter has an energy field and the energy that extends outwards can also be called our aura.

Our Aura is an Extension of Our Physical Body

When we meet each other, within seconds we will have an impression and can assess the kind of energetic vibe that is being given off. We'll assess if we are comfortable with this person or not, or what mood or frame of mind they might be in. This vibration can be felt subtly at times or there might be a greater presence about the person, given a stronger aura.

Some people have a strong personality, not necessarily always loud per say, and their aura can be more intense and can even extend out further from their bodies. Sometimes, without seeing or hearing them, we can feel people's auras when they come near us.

The auric field is made up of seven layers; each layer holds a different frequency because each of these layers is connected to different parts of us. This means each layer will receive information that comes from our physical self – from our organs, blood, bones, hair, skin and every other cell that makes up the human body. All of these parts are constantly sending and receiving information. These electrical and chemical intercommunications are being reflected out into each of the corresponding layers in this auric field.

Carolyn Myss, Ph.D. (1996) calls our surrounding auric field "a highly sensitive perceptual system." She agrees that all matter has an energy field because "everything is alive and pulsates with energy and all this energy contains information."

We are holistic beings, completely interconnected in that our physical functioning affects our emotions, minds and spirits – like an outer mood ring, if you will. Our auric layers will change their frequencies and colors as we shift and change our emotions, mental states and temperaments.

For example, as we make an emotional shift our aura will mirror out a higher vibration if we are feeling happy and well, or it will pulsate at a lower vibration if we are in a depressed or angry mood. Altogether, our auric field reflects our overall health, our personality and temperament, our beliefs, our mental activity and emotional state. It reflects everything going on with us, and this is where our "biography becomes our biology" (Myss, Carolyn 1996, p. 34)

Seeing an Auric Field

When our auric field can be read and interpreted by someone who is trained, it will also show where an imbalance or disease is present or is at risk of occurring. Unless we have learned to develop our natural "inner sight," or are a medical intuitive or clairvoyant, we generally do not physically see this energetic extension of our physical bodies, but we can certainly feel or intuit it. If we could all consciously see each other's electro-magnetic auric field it would measure about 3-9 feet around us, depending on the fluctuations of each person's degrees of health and wellness.

Many practitioners who work with healing the energies of the body, such as Reiki practitioners, become well developed in their intuitive abilities in sensing the auric field and sometimes can also see it. Most experienced energy healers will, at minimum, pick up the energies emanating from the auric layers in the field and will be able to intuitively interpret the body's energetic data being expressed through this field. They will be able to sense the areas of strength or depletion in the layers of the auric field and offer ways the client's body can be strengthened towards healing.

I have on some occasions seen aspects and colors of people's auric fields. These experiences began to occur more often when I was first involved in spiritual/energy studies, as well as in situations during my regular practice as a social worker over the years.

In one experience, I clearly saw the entire auric field surrounding one of my spiritual teachers become predominantly emerald green. It was so large and visible it consumed her entire energy field. This occurred as she and I were involved in very intense heart-centered meditation and we were calling in maximum healing energy to be involved in our meditation. It was a powerful moment for me to witness. The energy that filled the room was exceedingly peaceful, loving and calm.

In another situation whereby I was in a professional meeting, I witnessed the energy of a colleague flow right across the length of a long table to touch the energy field of another practitioner she was speaking to. It was immediately clear to me that this colleague's words carried more energetic impact in that moment because her mindful words in being solution focused were also infused with the compassion from her heart. This combination of heart-informing- mind is where wisdom lives. I have had other instances where I have seen the grace of the energy of white light come over a person's auric field. This light tells me they are in a very open state and are receiving and reflecting a higher vibration of energy coming from a greater source.

Auric Layers

The following diagram gives a visual idea of our outer auric field of energy and what each layer means from the first layer, closest to the body to the outermost seventh layer.

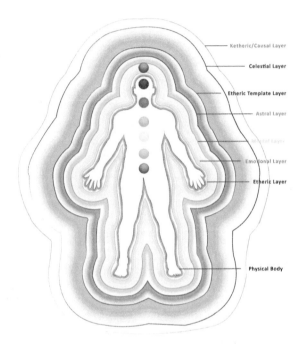

First Layer (Etheric Layer)

This layer (red in color) is closest to the physical body and it is really a subtle form of the physical body. The energies of this layer are awakened for the physical body through practices like yoga, tai chi, Qi gong, or by simply paying close attention to the energies, especially the breath.

Second Layer (Emotional Layer)

The Emotional Body (orange in color) is connected to our feelings, and it can change colors in rainbow-like fashion, according to the changing feelings of the person.

Third Layer (Mental Layer)

The Mental Body (yellow in color) holds our thoughts and mental processes. The primary color associated with this layer is yellow and can be seen more around the upper body with the head and shoulders.

Fourth Layer (Astral Layer)

This green colored layer acts as a bridge to the spiritual plane. The colors of the rainbow are present within this field of energy but can be seen as mostly a pink hue if the person is involved in loving, healing work. This level is also the emotional level that connects it to the heart chakra and emotional body.

Fifth Layer (Etheric Template Layer)

This blue colored layer can be seen by those gifted with clairvoyance as a deep blue and is closely related to the throat chakra.

Sixth Layer (Celestial Layer)

The Celestial Body (indigo blue in color) is related to the sixth chakra or third eye (or "mind's eye" of inner knowing or perception) and it is associated with spiritual enlightenment, unconditional love for humankind, intuition, and higher degrees of feelings and thoughts.

Seventh Layer (Ketheric/Causal Layer)

The seventh and violet colored layer is the body that contains all other bodies within it. This layer is associated with Universal or Divine Mind, serenity, and it contains all the information of the soul's journey through all of time (what is referred to as the Akashic Records).

As you can see, the auric field involves the psychological mind, our emotional natures, the physical body and our spiritual selves. From a Systems Theory perspective, what affects one part of our selves affects all the other parts. As vibrational beings, we inherently strive for an energetic balance or equilibrium. Being balanced is what we actually feel when we are in a place of calm and peace. Given the stresses of the world, we know that balance can be difficult to achieve at times let alone maintain.

Now we will look at the master whirling engines of our human system, our chakras – specific and highly sensitive energy vortexes strategically located within our body to disseminate information around the body and through to our auric field.

(For various examples of the colors noted in our auras, please see www.violet-aura.com)

Chakra Centers

"Chakras are energy-awareness centers. They are the revolving doors of creativity and communication between spirit and the world."

– Michael J. Tamura

In the ancient Eastern language known as Sanskrit, chakra means "the wheel." Chakras are considered to be the major energy centers of spiritual power in the body. Chakras do not fluctuate in their location. They remain stationary in our body and distribute life energies throughout our body and also connect through to our auric field.

In India, Ayurvedic, or life-knowledge medicine, observes illnesses in the body that are related to chakra imbalances, blockages or misalignments. When our chakras are not spinning properly in a clockwise direction, it can cause us to experience a level of discomfort, a result of our natural spiritual connection to life and our life force, or Chi, being slowed down.

This lack of Chi in our vibrational system can be felt in our physical energies being slow and lethargic, a sense of depression and even disconnection with ourselves and others. We can also feel a lack of cognitive clarity, inability to feel happiness, or experience a lack of self-esteem and self-confidence. This kind of situation can place anyone in a far more vulnerable place to turn to addictive substances to boost their low energies in more artificial ways.

The chakras are always in motion and the speed at which they rotate varies according to the state of health of each person. Each of our chakras is prescribed a dominant color that has a similar vibration as the chakra itself. Specific crystals, musical tones and even fragrances have vibrational measures that match each of the seven chakras. Each chakra has a connection to an organ as well as to one of the endocrine glands (Wills, 1993). The specific colors assigned do not mean that they are always actually seen as such. Many healers strongly intuit the chakras instead of seeing them in their color hues.

There are found to be distinct chakra purposes and effective ways of healing these energy centers to allow them to move properly when they have been interrupted by an emotional, physical, or mental event causing an imbalance or illness. Overall, when we exhibit a physical illness, it most often will first have been experienced as a spiritual or emotional disturbance, an unresolved hurt, injury or trauma. This disturbance will not only slow down any of the chakras, but its impact will also make its way through to our outer body's auric energy field.

The seven main chakras shown in the graph below are referenced most often in literature in terms of how they connect to our other energy systems, and how they can reflect imbalances that can potentially lead to ill-health or disease.

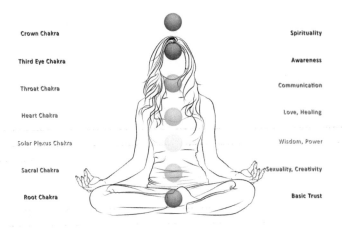

Crown Chakra — Spirituality

Third Eye Chakra — Awareness

Throat Chakra — Communication

Heart Chakra — Love, Healing

Solar Plexus Chakra — Wisdom, Power

Sacral Chakra — Sexuality, Creativity

Root Chakra — Basic Trust

First Chakra (Root) is red in color and the focus is with energies that feel vital and active.

Physical: adrenal glands for the flight-or-fight response, immune system, the base of our spine, rectum, legs, feet.

Imbalances: lethargy, sluggish or emotionally or physically inflamed, angry, depressed inability to focus.

Second Chakra (Sacral) is orange in color and involves our gut or intuitive feelings, sensuality, inner wisdom, curiosity, joyfulness, appropriate boundaries with parents.

Physical: colon, bladder and gall bladder, pelvis, sexual organs, hip, appendix and also adrenals.

Imbalances: mood swings, excessively strong emotions, disconnection from core self.

Third Chakra (Solar Plexus) is yellow in color. Its primary focus is the sense of "I" in our use of the intellect, knowledge and sense of our strength of will, our self-assertion and personal power.

Physical: digestive systems, liver, pancreas, middle back and muscles.

Imbalances: diabetes, chronic fatigue, hypertension, sarcasm, blaming and confused thinking.

Fourth Chakra (Heart) is green in color and is critically and centrally located and acts as a linkage between chakras one to three and four to seven. This chakra's focus is on healing, wholeness, a sense of something greater than ourselves, love, transformation, serenity, ability for insight, relationship connectedness, compassion, and empathy.

Psychological: a shut down or blocked heart chakra will become critical, judgmental, jealous, cold, too self-sacrificing.

Physical: heart, circulatory system, cardiac nerves, lungs, thymus, breasts, chest area, arms.

Imbalances: heart disease or attack, lungs, immune system, upper body pain.

Fifth Chakra (Throat) is blue in color and is concerned with communication, oration, voice resonance, truth telling, deeper listening, peace, and calm.

Physical: throat, thyroid, neck, parathyroid, mouth, teeth, and cervical spine.

Imbalances: all areas mentioned; communication issues - verbal domination, confusing messages, falsehoods and blocked creativity.

Sixth Chakra (Third Eye) is in indigo color and allows for heightened sensitivity, insights and integration between the observable and the unseen worlds, imagination, visualization, strength in mental clarity, and focus. The pineal gland is widely known as the seat of the soul and is the size of a small pea located centrally in the brain. It deals with the brain's functions, pituitary and pineal glands, overall head, eyes, and nose.

Imbalance: memory loss, lack of perception and objectivity, delusion, obsession, and emotional imbalance.

Seventh Chakra (Crown) is violet in color and is our welcoming, open connection to the Divine, Infinite Spirit and cosmic oneness in spiritual consciousness. It is ultimately about our ability to become energetically balanced and to attain unity and reconciliation within us and with all opposite forms of life, composing varying degrees of female and male energies (yin and yang). This reconciliation of energies is sought in order to allow a complete sense of love, peace, and harmony. In keeping this chakra open, we remain curious and alive in life's learning. Physically: involves our brain, cerebral cortex, skeletal system, and skull.

Imbalance: brain tumor, autism, crown headaches. Ego's domination in any area, greed, emotional dissociation, apathy, depression, and feeling ungrounded.

Whether we are able to see, sense or simply just appreciate the fact that we are and have a highly sensory and intelligent energy system embodied within each of us, it can support us in our self-care when we feel out of balance. When we have felt out of balance, many of us have sought energy treatments or vibrational medicine, without naming it in this way, to help us to rebalance. I have continuously received healing Reiki and all the other forms of vibrational medicine to re-balance my chakra system and treat or heal other stress-related issues when they occur.

(For examples of the colors noted in our chakras, please see 'Reiki in Adelaide' www.leisatimms.com)

Vibrational Medicine for Self-Care and Healing

"The natural healing force within us is the greatest force in getting well."
– Hippocrates, Father of Medicine.

Energy is also medicine. Many people without naming it have received vibrational medicine or some form of vibrational treatment. In recognizing ourselves as beings composed of energy, Gerber (2001) states, "vibrational medicine uses specialized forms of energy to positively affect those energetic

33

systems that may be out of balance due to disease states." The essential goal of vibrational medicine is to use forms of energy to move, unblock or rebalance our own body's energy to prevent illness or to eradicate disease.

Within our more traditional medical systems, practitioners like physiotherapists use vibrational energy in the use of electromagnetic energy in ultrasound to provide an energy balm for sore muscles and often combine it with transcutaneous electrical nerve stimulation (TENS) for pain reduction.

Vibrational medicine in radiation (electromagnetic waves) is used to kill some forms of cancer cells. Ultrasound waves are used to decrease the healing time for soft tissue inflammation in the post-acute phase by increasing the blood flow to the injured area, as well as increasing the production of more collagen to positively affect the formation of scar tissue, according to Sportsinjuryclinic.net (2016).

Vibrational medicine is also used to surgically remove malignant organs or tissue. Lasers are also used in eye surgery. Most recently, vibrational energy treatments have been adopted within the cosmetic industry for hair removal, fat-cell reduction and all manner of facial and body skin treatments.

Practiced on a regular basis, our daily self-care can affect any of our five senses. Some of these treatments are easy and available to calm and/or energize:

- Soothing musical tones
- Practicing simple meditation
- Aroma essences that are comforting and uplifting such as rose oil (antidepressant) or lavender oil (relaxation), jasmine and vanilla (for grief), as some examples
- Spending time in sunlight to boost serotonin levels
- Incorporating more natural, living, whole foods such as greens and fruits in daily nutrition
- Walking in the nourishing vibration of nature
- Drinking more water
- Adopting more regular physical movement and exercise during the day
- Positive self-talk by speaking to and about yourself with loving kindness, compassion, and encouragement

- Spending time with animals who offer unconditional love energy

Examples of vibrational energy healing techniques that have often been considered as the first order of care in other cultures are itemized below:

Reiki

The Japanese originated the practice of Reiki as a touch therapy using specific hand positions held above or on the body. Reiki works in support of all body systems and it is particularly powerful in balancing the chakra vortexes when they are out of balance and re-establishing the energy flow that in turn assists in all aspects of our healing.

Acupuncture

Acupuncture is thought to be 3,000 years old and originated in China. Acupuncture stimulates the body's own healing processes by using very fine needles gently placed into the skin on selected acupoints on the body.

Reflexology

Reflexology assists in the body's own healing processes and has some variance in its use by Western and Eastern cultures. It is a touch therapy that acts to prevent illness or respond to physical or emotional distress. Reflexology utilizes specific reflex points found in hands, feet, and ears that have corresponding nerve pathways or meridians connecting to all parts of the body.

Breathwork

There are many forms of vibrational medicine healing therapies that involve breathwork. Specific patterns of breathing exercises are incorporated into different practices to enhance the participants' complete holistic health. Forms of yoga and Tai Chi also use breathwork to improve self-awareness and mental and emotional issues.

Homeopathy

Homeopathic remedies are actually diluted doses of natural substances that are effectively used to cure the same symptoms that they can cause. This method of treatment stimulates the body's own healing mechanisms.

Flower Essence

Flowers and plants each have a specific, positive energetic frequency and, as such, the flower essence preparations are made to encapsulate the frequency that can assist in specific healing of the individual. Additionally, this preparation enhances the positive consciousness of the person in their connection with nature.

Healing Sound Therapies

Sound therapy or sound healing involves the human voice, as in chants, drumming, Tibetan singing bowls, tuning forks and gongs all for the purpose of vibrationally stimulating the natural healing energy of the body. Instead of traditional surgery using cutting procedures, surgeons in London have already used sound waves deep in the brain to help relieve a patient of his Parkinson's tremors. There will be more of these kinds of treatments to come.

Colored Light

Each color has a different wavelength and therefore a different frequency. Color is used in many ways to enhance our emotional, physical, and mental energies. The use of color in effective and multi-purpose ways to help in our care and healing is discussed at length in chapter 3.

Crystals or Gemstones

Crystals, or gemstones, have found their way back into our consciousness to advance healing and health practices recently, though they have been utilized since ancient times. Crystals hold higher vibrational frequencies than other stones and are also important conduits of energy, as we see with the use of them in our various technologies. The use of crystals and stones is discussed at greater length in chapter three.

To sum up, it makes sense as vibrational beings that we are open to consider the full range of proven vibrational medicine and treatment methods that can align with all of the body's intelligent network of cells, energy centers and fields to balance, heal and maintain our health. I believe we can easily see that the future of medical treatments and healing methods will use sound and light waves to a greater extent with success, and resulting in less intrusion for patients.

Chapter 2
Our Body's Wisdom

"Everything you need to know is within you. Listen. Feel. Trust the body's wisdom."

– Dan Millman

As we now appreciate that any words, beliefs or actions we hold true about ourselves is continuously being reflected in our body's experience, we can become actualized in our approach to health. It is important to try to be conscious about what we are actually saying - not only to ourselves in how we feel about who we are, but also how we feel specifically about our own bodies.

We know our bodies are an intelligent interconnected energy system. Our cells too are intelligent and aware of us in ways we may not normally have considered. Our bodies have wisdom and are indeed listening, taking in everything and everyone we encounter, including all experienced environmental stimuli, visual images and even those images created from within our own imaginations.

According to Pert (2008-2016), science is now proving that each and every cell in the body carries full memory of every single thing we have ever thought and experienced as well as the compaction of unresolved issues still festering away as they wait to be released.

Barbara Hoberman Levine (1991) in *"Your Body Believes Every Word You Say"* states our body is truly an emotional barometer. She posits that discomfort within our bodies can, at minimum, initially point to an area of emotional distress. Our bodies will never lie to us. That is why in order to find answers we can also look within and fine-tune listening to how our bodies are feeling.

38

Our bodies are always responding when we are able to pay attention to the signals. From chapter one, we can say, as example, if we are in an acute or prolonged state of stress of any kind, our bodies will begin to signal that stressful discord with aches, pains, nervous energy, sleep disruptions and, later on, with a more pronounced set of responses and symptoms to tell us to take action to alleviate or resolve our imbalance or disease.

Our spiritual, emotional, intellectual and physical realms are in constant intercommunications showing us the immense interweaving of the intelligence that we are. It also allows us to know that the more holistically aware we are the more we can consciously influence positive change within ourselves and in our bodies, regardless of our genetic makeup.

Cellular Knowledge

Science is recognizing that genes do not control all of the characteristics of our lives and are not the equivalent of the cell's brain. Recently, the biological science called epigenetics is being embraced and is showing us that cellular behavior is most profoundly influenced and even altered (without changing the genetic code) by our conscious beliefs as well as the environment in which they exist.

This cellular intelligence is not held within the nucleus, as one might assume, but rather in the membrane surrounding the cell, which directly receives signals from our environment and the impact of our beliefs. Environmental signals include all of the environmental, bio-psycho-socio-cultural influences and patterns in our lives expressed in our overall lifestyles.

Bruce Lipton (2008), renowned for his scientific research in the area of epigenetics, supports earlier civilizations' long-held spiritual and esoteric worldviews that all matter has, at its most basic elemental core, a consciousness, intelligence or spirit that underlies its behavior. The wisdom of the body is very real. This more recent and profound scientific view tells us that rather than being controlled or even victimized by what has been passed down to us in our genetic code, we can make choices in our environment and take greater mastery over our genes.

Lipton argues that changes in our minds, beliefs and visions of our world, leads to chemical changes in our blood, which ultimately control our genetics. The conscious intelligence of our cellular bodies and their interrelationship with our spiritual, emotional and psychological selves can be more clearly recognized.

With this recognition, it is far easier to appreciate that there are entire cellular communities within us, consciously performing specific jobs and responding continuously to the impact of our thoughts, words, sounds, as well as ingested food, air, water, the influence of others, and even the fabric and colors we wear. Our bodies are fully responsive to all our senses and to all of the energies with which we are involved.

Because we are energetic, vibrational beings, our understanding of the brilliance of our bodies' intelligence and capacities holds the potential for more miraculous breakthroughs in the healing arts and medical fields. Barlett (2007) emphasizes that the information coming forward via epigenetics and matrix energetics and many other interrelated fields, is not really new information at all, but rather ancient, spiritual and shamanic information being rediscovered and brought into our present-day consciousness.

Cellular communities with a purpose is a micro definition of who most of us are as complete whole beings, naturally part of our own collection of social and functional networks and communities, contributing to our sense of purpose and happiness. Barrett (2013) also tells us that each of our cells experiences its own purpose and reason to be a part of the particular community in which it thrives.

This understanding that cells are conscious and aware of their own purpose can be superimposed on a much larger scale that purports that cells in all living organisms on this planet are in fact sentient. Being sentient means having the ability to feel, perceive, or experience their existence subjectively – ergo, all of life is truly energetically alive.

If we consider this vital awareness of life being so dynamically alive in whatever energetic form, it gives rise to many issues including how we can consciously positively message our bodies to assist ourselves in every area possible. It means for example, we can be more conscious in preparing our bodies for surgery, recovery and self-care afterwards. The messages we give our cells in terms of what is going to happen, where the cells in our body parts are to be taken, and countless other considerations can help us.

This information is not so different in terms of how we would treat giving vital information to a person who is about to undergo a medical procedure, or how clients are to participate in their own heath care planning to optimize their recovery. In other words, verbally communicating with our body as a means of supporting our own health is not a crazy or out-there thing to do. Dangeli (2007-2017) calls it a direct form of bio-communication between you and your own body.

Body Talk

Earlier in my life, I had to undergo hip surgery and I decided to fully prepare myself for this surgery in all ways possible. I researched the procedure and spoke to my body about it. I explained exactly what was to take place. I asked my body to prepare to say good-bye to the part of my hip that was worn out. I thanked my body and hip for taking me as far as it did throughout my life, and to accept the new cellular material that was going in surgically. It was a conversation with myself similar to planning with a family to accept a newly adopted member with loving support.

In the course of that preparatory time, I developed my own pre-surgery and post-surgery visualizations, along with healing colors that I could use afterwards to ensure I could heal as fully as possible. I also sent prayers and did visual work in advance to assist the surgeons and all medical staff that they be guided and supported in their work. I have continued to talk and journal to my body whenever I feel the need to enquire about an organ or muscle and to encourage any needed healing.

An interesting, extensive study by Fosar and Bludorf (2011) states that we can create positive physical effects by using our own language with simple words and sentences. Their research further purports that, "This finally and scientifically explains why affirmations, autogenous training, hypnosis and the like can have such strong effects on humans and their bodies. It is entirely normal and natural for our DNA to react to language" (pdf. par. 5).

On a daily basis, where most of us are not involved in such scientific DNA cellular research, we can at minimum appreciate the immense wonder of our incredible capacity to holistically recover. We can heal more effectively from illness and surgery and assist in our holistic self-care by simple speaking lovingly and supportively to our body and tuning in to listen for its messages to us.

Made of Water

Being aware of thinking and speaking lovingly to our bodies becomes more conscious when we also recognize that we are primarily composed of water. Our water composition has implications. In 1999, Dr. Masuro Emoto authored an insightful book called *Messages from Water* in which he described experiments that had water droplets frozen and then analyzed their crystalline structure. Prior to freezing, each separate amount of water droplets was offered a loving word or conversely, a negative word or phrase.

Later, when examined microscopically, the droplets that had loving words imparted to them exhibited beautifully formed snowflake crystalline designs. The droplets exposed to negative words showed chaotic and disorganized particle structures. The water cells were obviously affected according to the energy of words given to them.

As simple as this experiment sounds, it is also worth paying attention to when we know we are composed of 92 percent water. It tells us of the importance of thinking and speaking with kindness, caring and love to our bodies – the very kind of words we would give to a dear friend.

Listening to Your Body's Messages

By accepting that our bodies really are listening to us, it can be helpful to be as understanding and compassionate about ourselves as possible. Most of us feel, unfortunately that we have some significant physical imperfection we need to hide or change and our body feels the thoughts of rejection we send it. The misperceptions and societal distortions we have as men and women have contributed to creating this distance from our own genuine remarkableness. It's also taken us away from the truth of our body's wisdom and our connection to the divine.

Looking into the Mirror

As a simple suggestion and initial practice on a daily basis, try this when you look into a mirror:

See your own reflection without judgment, condemnation or rejection. Thank your body and tell your body, "I accept you and I love you" for everything it has given to you. As you have already travelled some distance in this world in your physical vehicle, your body is really an invaluable friend – even if you feel it has confused you or you've not understood its messages. When you give your body these simple messages of acceptance and caring that your body deserves to hear, it will be a good thing.

Checking In With Your Body

Another simple exercise you can do is to check in with your body when you can. It takes a couple of minutes, at most. This check in can allow time for your body to give you direct information. Keep your expectations low in terms of receiving immediate inner verbal messages or images if you have never tried to communicate with your body before. You might only get subtle impressions or words as answers, but often all we really need is a word or a sense to tell us what we intuitively already know.

- First simply sit comfortably in your chair. Take in three deep breaths into your abdomen. For each breath, count to four as you slowly inhale, then hold your breath to the count of four, then exhale slowly to the count of eight.

Scan Your Body

- Mentally and emotionally scan your body beginning from the top of your head and go down your back and arms; check out your abdomen and your legs to your feet.

- Notice: where you are feeling tense, or have aches or pains. It's likely you already know why and where you hold tension in various areas. You may already know that your chair isn't ergonomically supportive to your body, or that the fluorescent lights are too hard on your eyes, or that you feel the strain of a very high work load and deadlines that feel nearly impossible to meet, or that there seems to be too much chatter around you to allow proper focus on your tasks.

  - Does your head ache? Do your eyes ache? Is your jaw clenched? Is your brow furrowed?
  - Where are your shoulders? Are they moving up towards your ears?
  - Are your hands clenched?
  - Is your stomach knotted?
  - How are your legs and feet feeling?
  - Is there an area in your body that holds the most tension, or do you experience your whole body as being constricted?

Ask Your Body

Approach your body with genuine concern and compassion. Ask your body, what does it need?

- Physically, is it hungry or thirsty? This may sound simple, but a lack of good routine nourishment or hydration will in itself create an energy drain followed by other mental and emotional symptoms.
- As you focus on your abdomen, ask "What do I feel, and what do I need?"
- Thank your body for communicating its messages.

Writing to Your Body

Another exercise is to simply write down a question to your body, a specific body part, or organ to receive an answer as to what is going on with it. What it is trying to tell you? Why it is in discomfort or pain? People have written to their lungs, kidneys, legs, and other parts of their bodies, and have received information. You may get inner impressions, emotional insights or feelings that can be emotionally painful events from the past that may be still affecting you and are manifesting physically. Aside from dialoguing directly with your body, writing or journaling is an effective way to allow information to come forward from your body.

Each of our bodies holds clear wisdom through our cellular memories and also through its immediate responses to people, places and things that come onto our path. Our body remains our truth barometer, or ultimate lie detector, and it will always tell us in some way what is going on in any situation, negatively or positively?

In any moment, you can experience your body's messages by simply consciously focusing and tuning into your body, specifically your solar plexus, as your gut-sense barometer to feel your way through situations. Even if your head cannot figure out what is happening, if something doesn't feel right and if your gut sense tells you that something isn't safe, then that more intuitive part of you is what you need to heed. I have heavily relied on my intuitive sense my entire life because it too is a faithful messenger.

Clarifying our Natural Spiritual Senses

"People have always understood intuitively that mind and body are not separable. Modernity has brought with it an unfortunate dissociation, a split between what we know with our whole being and what our thinking mind accepts as truth. Of these two kinds of knowledge the latter, narrower, kind most often wins out to our loss" (Mate, 2012, p. xi).

Within the richness of our humanness, we all have natural spiritual gifts with which we arrive. We may have suppressed, denied, or acculturated to regard our sensory gifts as part of our own so-called crazy imaginations. Some people believe our extrasensory natures to be a negative aspect of who we are that needs to be expunged. Thankfully, our natural human senses are being accepted and expressed more openly to give all of us a chance for more personal exploration and development.

Being part of the animal kingdom, we are sentient beings, - meaning we are naturally intuitive beings. Those who have more developed intuition can also have several sensory gifts available to them when receiving extraordinary information. This information can come from within from our inner or higher selves, or as some would believe our guides, the angelic realm or even deceased loved ones spiritually existing in another dimension on the other side.

Where these messages come from is up to us to discern. For many people who have not really had exploration in these areas, we still can experience these kinds of messages or information at various times and remember them as curious, minor events. Or, perhaps they may have been profound moments that touched our hearts, opened our minds, and offered a rich glimpse into another realm available to us.

My strong belief based on my own experiences is that the more we value our spiritual senses and fully understand them, the more information we can bring in to guide our own lives. I have benefited enormously from listening to my body, my intuition and my other senses described below. This kind of honoring, listening and following creates more strength in us as we learn to trust ourselves more deeply.

Honoring Our Intuition

In essence, intuition is also referred to as our higher instinct and is part of our survival senses. It also means knowing without really knowing, sensing something might happen in a certain way, or that we need to take a certain action, without being able to articulate exactly how or why that knowing exists. When we have ignored our gut sense, our instinctual intuition, we might have heard ourselves saying, "I knew I should have done that. Why didn't I listen?" We've often regretted it!

There are times when I want to make a decision, but I am hampered by this sense of knowing something is really off. I cannot put my finger on it, and it's as if I am stuck. It's not necessarily from being afraid of making the wrong decision. It usually means that the timing of the decision is off in terms of other events behind the scenes being formed and lined up in my life, or there is a lack of information to allow me to decide what to do – in that either it's not yet evolved naturally forward, or I have not made enough effort to seek it out.

Along with our intuition there are other natural spiritual gifts that we have. You may resonate to any of the following:

Clairaudience

Clairaudience means clear hearing. It is our ability to receive words and sounds that are not part of the regular sensory realm. Hearing specific sounds or voices or music that is not discernable to the normal ear. Clairaudient information is received mentally or literally within the ears. For example, when I was a new motor vehicle driver I was driving alone and about to turn left onto another street that was not frequently busy. Just before I made the turn, a very loud voice shouted on my right side, "Don't turn!" It really startled me, but made me hesitate for a just a second, only to see a speeding car narrowly miss me as it suddenly appeared from nowhere and turned right into my path. We would have had a terrible head-on collision if I'd continued with the turn.

Clairsentience

Clairsentience is a clear feeling where one is able to discern at a distance another's state of feeling with no plausible explanation as to how it can be known. This extrasensory ability can occur when we have a strong, distinct feeling blanket us without explanation, feelings we can also experience on a physical level. This kind of experience has been well documented over time and often comes up between parent and child or loved ones who are at a distance and an illness or injury has occurred. I can attest I have had countless experiences like these with family members, friends, and animals.

Clairvoyance

Clairvoyance is clear seeing or vision where one is able to gain information about a person or situation that is at a distance through visual telepathy. It is also referred to simply as extrasensory perception (ESP). One of the most famous clairvoyants in our history was Edgar Cayce, (1877-1945) who exhibited profound abilities while in deep sleep and trance states. His work has continued to be studied to this day.

Claircognizance

Claircognizance is clear knowing and is more than intuitiveness. It is a very developed sense of knowingness that transcends time and can allow a person to access information about a person or situation in the past, present, and future. It can involve predictions, or premonitions and flashes of immediate insights that cannot be backed up with any concrete explanation. This is a spiritual gift that I have found within myself that has risen up since my early days, quietly but significantly. The information arises as needed and as one is ready to receive it. As forms of meditation and relaxation enhance all spiritual insights, it also enhances claircognizance.

A simple example is while I was relaxing with a friend years ago, I suddenly knew in a moment that "my mother is going to pass away in two weeks." My mother lived at a distance and there was no evidence given her relative youthfulness to suggest her death would be imminent, but she died from a sudden heart attack exactly to the day two weeks after I said it. The knowing as I can best describe it, is a clear whole-being or body-mind-spirit kind of experience and feels irrefutable when the sensory information comes through me. There are other examples that have occurred over time but this insight was one of the most startling for me.

I constantly rely on the breadth of my intuitive senses and I will always strive to listen and develop them. Overall, I can say with absolute certainty that when we give all of our senses the attention and validation they deserve we will strengthen our capacity to provide ourselves with more accurate information. When we are inquisitive about our 'extraordinary', yet wholly natural senses and tune in to them more closely and consistently, many more decisions become easier and clearer and our lives can run more smoothly.

There are informal and formal ways to develop our additional senses. There are credible institutes that offer formal trainings, such as the Arthur Findlay College in Stansted, England that I had opportunity to attend. There are many others locally and worldwide that offer a range of structured retreats and inner journeying with excellent teachers to bring forward one's spiritual development. There are so many things we can do easily on a daily basis through spiritual groups, personal meditations, any creativity or art work, music, play and spending time with animals or being out in our natural surroundings. All of these and more that will stimulate and enhance our spiritual senses.

Managing Levels of Sensitivity

As we appreciate that each of us is uniquely expressively different, many people feel curious to acquire more learning and validation about their own personality aspects, communication styles, preferences, and sensory sensitivities.

There are countless formal and informal tests and questionnaires available that range from assessing superficial aspects of individuals to those assessments that are far more in depth and comprehensive. Popular personality assessments are easily accessible online, but may not be reliable. Numerous online quick questionnaires can be found that purport to test for various sensitivities such as empathy that offer only a cursory analysis of some of those qualities.

People who experience the world in more sensorial acute ways who also might be more gifted, in some of the "claire" areas we've mentioned can also at times react in ways that can be confusing to themselves and others, contributing to unfortunate misunderstandings. Withdrawal, retreat, nervousness, getting overwhelmed, and agitated, immune system issues, allergies and other associated symptoms can be a few signs of extra sensitivities that need more attention and support. It's to our benefit to know how to recognize our areas of sensitivities, and if there are areas we need to manage, protect, or heal. It is also well worth exploring if there are additional traumatic experiences adding to any of our responses or triggered reactions.

An excellent read I would recommend for more personal self-exploration in this area is, *The Highly Sensitive Person, How to Thrive When The World Overwhelms You*, (1996) by Elaine Aron. This author provides a professional and personal depth of understanding of the sensitivities that we all possess, but gives needed focus for the highly sensitive person (HSP) to embrace, cope and thrive with their degrees of sensitivities with good strategic self-care methods.

Specifically, sensitive, intuitive, empathic people have the ability to quickly feel and absorb others' emotions. These people are found in all walks of life and occupations, as one would guess, and those of us that experience our senses acutely need to manage+ our intuitive empathic natures well in stressful environments or in roles that are less geared to be "feeling focused". You'll usually find intuitive empaths gravitate more towards the healing arts or helping occupations that allow for easier self-expression and acceptance.

Highly sensitive people will sometimes take more time to reconcile their desire to seek advancement into leadership roles for example. The reason is that they can perceive, rightly or not, that there could be an increase in degrees of stress and subsequent feelings of becoming overwhelmed when facing situations with more wear and tear to the nervous system.

Additionally, even if we consider the impact of social psychological, cultural and gender factors, sensitive people may experience lesser degrees of ego strength, because they may tend to focus on what they need to learn rather than appreciating wisdoms they have already acquired. This trait can be displayed in shyness, self-deprecation and self-consciousness. Ergo, they may feel they are less equipped to go forward when in fact their insights and inner wisdom offerings are what some organizations may really need.

An interesting conundrum is that in occupations like health care, education, social services and direct caregiving – where sensitive intuitives, healers and empathic people are liable to gravitate – these occupations are often cited as some of the highest stress positions for all levels of staff who are vulnerable to feeling overworked, overwhelmed, and subsequently burned out.

Markowitz (2013) argues that many empathic people will tend to mask, manage, or cope with their sensitive natures vis-a-vis the barrage of ongoing and cumulative levels of workplace stress by resorting to alcohol consumption and/or other drugs, including over-the-counter medications to deal with increased anxiety, stress-related nervous disorders, chronic fatigue and sleeplessness.

From my own perspective, most people are actually a lot more emotionally and sensory sensitive than they generally care to admit or openly discuss. This reticence can sometimes be a result of a cultural, gender, or work-setting issue, with men feeling withheld more than women to recognize or reveal their intuitive, empathic and sensitive natures.

Overall, managing our emotional sensitivities or some of the higher acute senses, remains an important focus for self-care. It's helpful if this care involves some knowledge about clearing and grounding our energies, as well as asserting our boundaries and other supportive protection measures, within our work or our home environments. Some of these strategies are addressed in chapters three and four.

Chapter 3
Grounding, Clearing And Raising Energy

"If every 8 year old in the world is taught meditation, we will eliminate violence from the world within one generation"
– Dalai Lama, 2012

Meditating is Easy

The benefits of practicing simple daily meditation have been well documented. These benefits include: grounding and calming the mind and nervous system, reducing stress, creating inner connections with one's self, shifting perceptions to allow for increased creative, innovative thoughts, expanding a loving connection with all life, and the list goes on.

Practicing meditation is actually very easy. It's about focusing and being present. For a long time, I didn't warm up to the notion of meditation until I realized I was already doing informal meditations – when I went into deeper conscious mind states when I wrote, painted, gave in-depth counselling sessions, and even quietly tuned into music.

Later on, when I began to take more formal meditations through my spiritual training courses, I found the restful clearing benefits became greatly enhanced. Once you decide on a time and place to practice meditation, you can easily develop it as a habit. The truth is you can meditate, as you need to – indoors or outdoors.

There are different kinds of meditations and one that is well known is called Transcendental Meditation, founded by the Indian Guru Maharishi Mahesh Yogi. It incorporates mantra or chanting that uses various energetic vibrations in sounds that can assist in opening us to different levels of consciousness. To develop the habit of being mindfully present, meditating in the morning is usually a good place to start.

There are many simple meditations that can be practiced daily whereby all you need is a quiet space for 2 -5-15 or 20 minutes, whatever works as a beginning point as well as for your schedule. Some people like to build up their meditation time and start at 2 minutes, then 5 minutes and on from there. In essence, meditation is about being focused and present while also focusing on your breath.

Quick-Start Meditation

Wherever you are that is comfortable and makes sense to refocus is fine. If you are outside you can also do this while walking.

Focus completely on your breath. If you want to take a few deep breaths to immediately calm you – you can, but in this exercise – if you only focus on your breathing in and out the moment – it's sufficient. Just continue to closely focus on your breath and as you do your mind will continue to want to chatter to you. Ignore the chatter and keep solely focused on your breath, in and out. Focus on your breathing for as long as you can – even if only for 10 – 30 seconds. It will still be very helpful to turn your attention inward and become quieter inside.

If you want to try another easy breath technique that uses a different rhythm to compare, I suggest Dr. Andrew Weil's 4-7-8 Breath Technique. He has a brief video offering a good example of a breathing technique that is simple and effective.

(*http://www.drweil.com/videos-features/videos/the-4-7-8-breath-health-benefits-demonstration/*).

Heart of Compassion Meditation

To me, in addition to focusing on my breath, I have also turned into my heart center as the most powerful energy center from which to begin. Our hearts can powerfully guide us in how we can compassionately and clearly move through this world to bring forward compassion and peace from within and then send that compassion out to others.

Some people like to light a white candle for a spiritual focus in meditation, but it is not always necessary for an effective meditation. If you want to keep your eyes open, then looking at a candle is an excellent focus point. If you are not in a place to use a candle, just choose another focus that has some kind of meaning reflecting love or nature.

1. You can sit in a chair or sofa, sit cross-legged on the floor, or fully lie down. If you choose to sit down, ensure your spine is straight with your legs on the floor and head positioned looking straight ahead for a good energy flow. Just be comfortable.

2. Place your hands palm up on your lap or in another mudra position. There are many positions to hold your hands and fingers for different meditations and they each hold meaning in their correspondence to various organs. As well as the intention for the meditation and the healing benefits that go with each one, there are many good websites to give you an idea of the sacred meaning of the mudras and one is: www.harisingh.com/news**Mudras**.htm.

For this meditation, you can use the Shuni Mudra as shown on the next page.

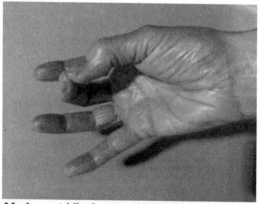

Shuni Mudra: *middle finger and thumb tips touch. Assists to help one remain present.*
(http://www.harisingh.com/newsMudras.htm)

1. Focus on your breath and inhale a deep slow breath (count from 1 to 4) in through your nose and then out through your mouth (count from 1 to 4). Do this 3 times.
2. Focus on your heart. Think of your heart having a beautiful slightly closed pink rose within it. Think of the animals and people you love. Send them your love and see your love for them being returned back to you – into your heart. As you breathe, continue to focus on this rose and see it slowly open up its petals. As it opens, it also opens you to receive more love, kindness, and compassion. Ask for love, kindness, and compassion for yourself and for all living beings.
3. See the loving pink energy from this rose expanding to include your whole heart, then further expanding to fill your whole body. Envision this pink, loving light energy now filling your room, home, or work setting, and then expanding to fill the whole building. Continue to visualize this healing pink light filling the entire neighborhood, then the country you live in, until you are able to visualize this energy completely surrounding our whole Earth.

The energy of the loving thoughts for yourself and extending towards others in this visualization is real. It is an extremely positive thing to do and it makes a difference in ways of which you may never be aware, but extending love, kindness and compassion is soothing and ultimately healing. Others do receive it, and as energy flows it will be returned to you again and again.

(Note: There are countless recorded guided meditations to follow without effort which you can purchase online or in local health or spiritual stores. They can be focused on a specific issue or just be a general relaxation tape).

Easy Grounding Activities – Get Physical

We contain earthly elements in our physical body and have the natural Earth's gravity to assist us in becoming consciously connected with our physicality; it allows for easier grounding. A few examples are:

- Have a massage
- Sit in water with Epsom salt, or simply shower
- Walk in nature
- Garden
- Work with clay, sand, or dirt
- Dance, run, walk vigorously
- Eat root vegetables
- House clean and de-clutter
- Go to sleep earlier for a longer rest
- Be with loving animals
- Roll a tennis ball under your feet

Clearing Energy

Are They Someone Else's or Mine?

Thoughts as sparks of energy can fly faster than a blink of an eye between one person and another. Watch what happens in any meeting or with anyone you're with and you will start to experience knowing exactly what is going to be said next. Sometimes this inner knowing is because we can sense the patterns of speech being used in our work arena, and other times we are simply quickly tuning in and receiving distinctive thoughts being sent out by those around us. You can easily try a quick experiment by repeating in your mind a distinct thought and sending it out into the room to see who picks it up.

This connection we have with each other through our thoughts and feelings can happen at a distance as well. Thoughts being energy has no trouble travelling through time and space in a millisecond. For example, when a major tragic event has occurred anywhere on the planet and large numbers of lives have been lost with ongoing trauma being experienced, we might not yet be aware of what has happened across the globe, but we will feel a collective sense of those energies to varying degrees.

We are also aware of those times when we suddenly think of someone out of the blue and they call us, or we connect with them and are told with surprise, "You have been on my mind", or "I was just thinking of you!" You can call this phenomenon a form of energy transference or telepathy since we are all telepathic, like other animal species in our world.

At times we can suddenly begin to feel drained, depressed, anxious and unmotivated. Sometimes we know exactly why we feel this way and other times it's not clear. These feelings can happen frequently when we have been in stressful situations and around others who are experiencing difficult circumstances, even if they are not telling us about them. We can also pick up a whole range of energies simply by travelling on public transit.

Our auric field is like a sponge and it can easily absorb the energies of those we interact with most often or most closely. Soaking up feelings and receiving others' thoughts can be an uplifting experience if we are around high-energy or positive souls, or it can be otherwise disconcerting. This absorption can also occur to such an extent that it becomes more challenging to differentiate between our own feelings and thoughts and those belonging to someone else. This is particularly true of caregivers, healers, or clinicians who work with people who are ill, dying or who are highly anxious in states of anger, grief, or depression.

A quick question to ask yourself when you suddenly feel down, sad, angry, out of sorts, or just off in some way with no immediate reason: *Are these thoughts or feelings someone else's or mine?* Then wait if an inner answer comes.

If you're still not clear, you can say: *If these thoughts or feelings of (anger, despair, sadness, etc.) are not mine, then I send them back to the Universe to be dissolved immediately.* Then see if your mood or thoughts shift.

Overall, no matter where we are – at work, home, a restaurant, in a movie or sports theatre, lecture hall, or on a bus or subway, there are energy states of others that we will absorb and hold in our own energy field. We then can become more easily physically and emotionally drained and not recognize why. When we become bogged down by the cumulative energies of others, it also becomes more difficult to hear our own inner voice or guidance, so it is important to check in and clear our energy field.

The Tree Root Visualization

1) **Begin by sitting comfortably in a chair** with both feet touching the ground. Focus on your breath. Inhale a deep slow breath (count to 8) in through your nose and out through your mouth (count to 8). Do this 3 times.

2) **Mentally scan your body** beginning from the bottom at your feet and working your way up to the top of your head, through your legs, back, front torso, arms, neck, and head. Take note of any areas of discomfort, tension or stress. Areas that feel to be in discomfort are signals there are blocked energies present that may need releasing and/or healing, through massage, physiotherapy, acupuncture, acupressure, Reiki, or other healing methods.

3) **Roots:** Imagine your feet have roots extending into the center of the earth. Anchor your feet's roots around the core of the earth and visualize Earth's energy coming back up through your feet, then up to your legs and encircle that energy around where your ovaries would be located as a woman, and as a man, where your testicles are.

4) **Long-Stemmed Rose:** Imagine a beautiful white long-stemmed rose above your head. Bring down pure white light from about 100 feet above your head, through the rose, and have it wash over and through your entire body. As a visual this would be like standing in a shower of beautiful white energy flowing around and through every cell of your body.

5) **Golden Rose:** Imagine you have a golden-colored rose that is available like a powerful vacuum cleaner. Visualize that golden rose encircling all around your auric field and completely sucking up any lingering energetic debris that has not been cleared away from the earlier white light. When you feel finished, take the golden rose and toss it out into space, and see it disintegrate completely into the purity of the Universe.

Clearing by Smudging

Smudging with the smoke of burning herbs, grasses, or with pre-constructed herbs in sticks of white sage, cedar, lavender, osha root, mugwort, or sweet grass is a beneficial way of clearing and cleansing away negative energies around you. Smudging comes from the First Nations or Native American healing and Shamanic traditions and recognizes our connection to the sacredness of plant energies.

Each plant or herb has its own unique qualities and offers up its intelligent, purifying, healing, and energizing benefits. Be aware of your intention when involved in smudging as you connect with and honor the plant's sacred healing qualities. In essence, individually, the practice of smudging around the body for cleansing holds that when burning certain herbs, the smoke will attach itself to the negative energies. As the smoke clears, so does the negative energy that had been present in the person's auric field.

The result is a feeling of being refreshed and energized. This is a good practice to have before an important event or after a depleting or emotionally draining experience.

To smudge yourself:

- Be clear about your intention to clear your mind and body of any negativity.
- Light the smudge stick (it is preferable to use a candle to light rather than a match or lighter).
- To cleanse yourself, blow out the stick and allow the stick to smolder.
- Fan the smoke with your hands or by using a feather and go from head to foot allowing the negative energy to flow out. Encourage it to wash over your body from atop your head, around your body, down to your feet, or vice versa.
- During this process, you can remain quiet in thought, speak your intentions, or voice a simple prayer.

There are those who prefer to practice smudging in a far more detailed and meticulous manner, but for quick ease in accomplishing what you want, the simpler method will still work well.

The Quick Clearing Technique:

If you're in a situation where you have little time and you might be in a more confined space, you can do the following in a minute or less:

Simply take both of your hands and run them just over your head, or even through your hair like a comb. Toss or flick off the energy away from yourself – (and not onto someone else!)

Then take your hands and go down your arms, torso, and legs. Take your right hand and run it down your left arm and over your hand, and flick the excess energy off from your left hand out to the universe. Do the exact same thing with your left hand, running it down your right arm and hand and flicking it out to the universe. Imagine a dust buster vacuum or golden rose and use it all around you to completely vacuum up any residual debris. Breathe deeply and put an egg shape of white light around you. Drink a glass of purified filtered or alkalized water.

Mind Clearing Command

The following excerpt is from John Randolph Price's 1981 book, *The Superbeings*. Understanding that our words have great power, I have used this command for many years with clear results. Once you say it (out loud is best, but not required), wait a minute or so and you can experience a shift to a clearer state of mind.

You can change the words to suit yourself. The important thing is that you know your word is stated for your own best interests, backed up by the depth of your feelings and harms no one. It therefore acts as a powerful clearing command. The "Law of Spirit", as Price refers to it in the quote, is really the creative force of Universal energy that surrounds us and is within us.

"I call on the Law of Spirit to clear out any thoughts in my consciousness mind that resemble fear, rejection, prejudice, inadequacy, impatience and criticism of myself or others. I don't need them, I don't want them and I command them gone."

Chakra Clearing Using Musical Tones and Crystals

"If I were not a physicist, I would probably be a musician. I often think in music. I live my daydreams in music. I see my life in terms of music".

– Albert Einstein

Music is a powerful universal language and there is ample proof that healing tones bring about a sense of balance and rejuvenation. Specific sounds, tones and their frequencies go hand in hand with chakra clearing, balancing, and healing. We actually know this instinctively when we are drawn to the sound of the soothing tone of someone's caring voice or the calming effect of music set in tonal frequencies that bring us a sense of calm and peace.

Many health care settings including post-operative acute care have utilized soothing vibrational music to heal, lower blood pressure, and boost immunity. We could certainly expand on using soothing tones in myriad ways in far more of our health care settings.

Crystal singing bowls have also been used for centuries for very effective chakra cleansing and balancing. The sounds are highly resonating and the results feel immediate. Many Reiki and other energy healers use crystal bowls in their daily work. If you have never heard the crystal bowls that are matched up with the chakra tones shown in the diagram below, you can listen to these tones by checking out sites that offer free recordings.

- *Meditation Freedom: Chakra Balancing and Healing Meditation Music with Crystal Bowls:* https://www.youtube.com/ Chakra Balancing and Healing Meditation Music with Crystal Bowls
- Steven Halpern's, "*Chakra Suite*": Halpern Inner Peace Music. www.StevenHalpern.com
- Chakra Healing Sounds, Dr. Jane Ma'ati Smith, C.HyP. Msc.D: http://balance.chakrahealingsounds.com/the-7-chakras

Crystals (or gemstones) and stones are also alive with the energy of the universe flowing through them and their natural healing and restorative properties have been used for centuries to help clear and rebalance chakras. During their work, energy healers will often place specific crystals and stones on the chakra centers to amplify the effectiveness of the healing.

Crystals in particular, aside from being powerful in their healing capacities are also used in countless technologies from watches to medical devices and electronics. There is a consciousness that we find when getting to know crystals meaning that when we understand the crystal kingdom being ancient and alive with Earth's evolving energy, we begin to develop a relationship with their powerful energetic essence as we do with the other natural inhabitants of our Earth.

For myself, I have a natural resonance for crystals. When I travelled to Egypt in 2005 with a spiritual group, I had the rare opportunity to sit in a healing circle in the King's Chamber within the Great Pyramid. I took quite a few large quartz crystals with me during that sitting and, to this day, they are still infused with powerful energy from my time there. *Crystal Therapy, How to Heal and Empower Your life with Crystal Energy* (Virtue, Doreen. and Lukomski, Judith. 2005) as well as *The Crystal Bible* (Hall, Judith. 2003) are excellent books for understanding the precious properties and sacred uses of rocks, crystals and minerals as well as their proper care.

The guide below shows the corresponding tones and crystals or gemstones associated with our primary chakra centers. A worthwhile small handbook for chakra clearing by Doreen Virtue (1998) is called *Chakra Clearing, Awakening Your Spiritual Power to Know and Heal.*

Chakras, Tones, Gems and Stones

Chakra	Tone	Gems and Stones
1. Root chakra: tourmaline	**C, C#**	**Garnet, onyx, red jasper** Focus: assists in spatial intuition

2. Sacral:	D, D#	**Carnelian, orange zincite** Focus: restoration of balance
3. Solar plexus	E	**Citron, tiger's eye, golden topaz** Focus: healing and teaching power
4. Heart:	F, F#	**Rose quartz, green tourmaline** Focus: clairsentience and intuition
5. Throat:	G, G#	**Turquoise, blue agate** Focus: expression
6. Third Eye:	A, A#	**Lapis lazuli, sodalite** Focus: clairvoyance
7. Crown:	B	**Amethyst, clear quartz** Focus: claircognizance

(Virtue, D. and Lukomski J. 2005 Crystal Therapy. How to Heal and Empower Your Life With Crystal Energy)

Etheric Cords

Cords are really energetic, emotional attachments that we make with others or others make with us, often unconsciously. They develop between us in order to provide a more psychic or speedier communication link. If you are clairvoyant, you can see cords appear as thin dark tubes coming out of a person's body.

They can be attached to specific chakra centers depending on the nature of the relationship. For example, some cords between romantic or intimate partners are seen being attached to all or some of the chakras, or generally specifically to the heart chakra and to the second (sexual) chakra. Those attachments can be negative or positive depending on the quality of the relationship.

Positive cords are natural and are found between those in loving relationships, such as with spouses, parents, children, or close friends. These cords run energy between people that feels uplifting and strengthening.

Negative cords are created when we find ourselves in relationships with people who have a reliance upon us that is primarily fear based. In other words, they are afraid if you leave they will lose their source of complete happiness. We often find strong cords between addicted and co-dependent people and their spouses or family members. This kind of energetic over-attachment can drain your energy leaving you feeling fatigued.

In the helping professions, fear-based cords and other cords that can attach to you from within angry or grief-laden atmospheres are common between clinicians and with those connected to them. There is nothing inherently wrong with a healthy clinician/client relationship when the boundaries and expectations are clearly defined and followed.

However, in spite of that, there are times when a person being assisted by a clinician will develop an over-attachment when they have not yet developed or strengthened their own core sense of self, or when their health is so compromised that the idea of the clinician or healer leaving them becomes extremely distressing.

There is no judgment about this situation. As human beings we can all go through experiences whereby we feel needy or have been seriously injured in some way that we require extra support to heal. We will experience levels of dependency and that is part of our own natural experience towards deeper growth. All of us in these extraordinary times can develop an over-attachment, even if short lived. Still, cord cutting is a good idea and does not need to come from a negative intention. It just needs to come from your own awareness that you are doing something out of self-regard in respecting that you are responsible for taking good care of your energy.

Cord Cutting

One of the ways we can detach with love and respectfully assist in clearing and protecting ourselves is to often do an energetic cord cutting. Some people who work extensively with others who are in need of healing use cord cutting daily as a matter of discipline to keep their own energy clear. Cord cutting does not destroy a relationship that still has growth involved, but it does serve to energetically eradicate unhealthy aspects of energy between people while maintaining the true loving connection. Any love that has truly existed between people is not destroyed because it is the energy that exists through all of time and space.

However, if it's best to be disconnected from that person the intelligent spiritual energy you have called upon will assist in creating more of a severance according to your best interests or highest vision. Be aware when you cut cords you may also find those people you are detaching from can psychically pick up the detachment without conscious understanding. They may possibly feel a sudden need to reconnect. Be prepared to set any needed boundaries should they contact you and keep the disconnection intact. The section on boundaries that follows in this chapter can be helpful during this process.

People can re-cord or reattach frequently. You don't necessarily need to know who the person is that has developed this attachment, you only need to do the following exercise for it to make a difference.

Cord Cutting Exercise 1.

1. Do one of the previously described grounding and clearing exercises first for your preparation.

Take a moment to again breathe deeply, inhale and exhale slowly 3 times and think of the person you want to clear from or from whom you wish to create distance.

Think of a large pair of scissors and imagine them cutting all cords that are around you, beneath your feet and above your head.

Imagine your auric field as clean and unattached from this person. As you release this person, ask that this person be blessed by God, the Angels or whomever you may wish to call on. You can also imagine pink light going towards them and surrounding them and bless them in their life's journey.

Say to yourself: "I release _____ from my life and I thank (God, Higher Power, Allah, Source, Spirit, Creator, my Higher

65

Self or ____) for the lessons I take with me. It is done and I am free."

Your words and your natural ability to visualize your declaration are powerful and commands that the Universe deliver, as you use your power in the right way.

Cord Cutting Exercise 2

Some people may not find the concept of a realm of etheric beings feels right for them. These concepts are for each of us to accept or reject. Author, psychologist and clairvoyant Doreen Virtue purports the power of the Angelic level in her life and has consciously raised the knowledge of this spiritual realm with her extensive writing to assist many people across the globe. In my own life, I have also gone through events that defy normal explanation when I have experienced moments of divine intervention. These were occasions when my life and the lives of those with me had been dramatically spared (Halcrow, 2011).

Below is an extrapolation of Doreen Virtue's (1999) suggestion in another cord cutting tool to release anyone who might be draining your energy. Simply say:

"Archangel Michael, I call upon you to severe the cords attached to anyone that is draining my energy. Please remove their cord and any fear or negativity they have brought to me."

With so many systemic changes and challenges, stresses can lead to feelings of frustration, moodiness, fear, and negativity. Combine those challenges with the small pod areas in which many people find themselves working so closely together and the result is a more pronounced buildup of negative energy. Clearing and raising our workspace energy is good to do.

Clearing and Raising Workspace Energy

Negative energy gets stuck in cluttered workplaces too because clutter creates energy blocks. It also gets stuck in our workspaces when tragedy or sadness begins to build up from many of the serious, depressing situations that colleagues, particularly in helping professions, need to debrief about. Even though it is helpful in the moment, the energy in that debriefing is still discharged into the environment and can remain. All thoughts, words and feelings are imprinted into our environment – the walls, chairs, rugs, whatever is visible or not so invisible. It all remains there until we consciously clear it away.

Strategies to clear and raise the vibrational levels in our work environments will always involve our human energetic selves in that our own frequencies in the end ultimately give rise to improved workspace feelings. They are inextricably linked. The suggestions below that affect us directly will also positively impact the environment.

Decluttering

First look to your own space and see if there is anything you can clear, re-organize or declutter. It is not surprising to see one clinician clearing her/his space followed by others. Setting the example can be psychologically encouraging because we instinctively know we feel better and work better in an organized space, even if it only lasts for a few days and we have to go at it again! Decluttering should be done on a routine, even weekly basis as a habit to make the positive energy setting in work for you.

Smudging the Environment

In a broader measure, depending on policies of your organization, it is useful to explore the use of smudging in your workspace. We know this is a powerful way of clearing our body's auric field and it can assist in clearing any environment. Of course one would have to perform this in a setting where windows could be opened to avoid smoke detectors from being triggered.

- It's a good idea is to individually smudge before your environmental smudge.
- Be clear about your intention to cleanse your space of negativity and follow the same process of lighting your herb.

- Pay attention to allowing smoke into corners, behind doors, closet spaces, window areas, and even around electronics.
- As above, during your individual smudge you can remain quiet in thought, speak your intentions, or voice a simple prayer.
- You can do this process of clearing your space as an individual, in a group, or splitting the group off into several areas.

Power in the Voice

As we're aware of specific vibrational tones to calm, heal, clear, and energize, we can also consider many benefits in using our voices singularly or collectively to raise our personal vibration and energy and extend that positivity to our home and workspaces by singing or chanting. The combination of sound, breath, and rhythm when practiced consistently changes our neurological systems in shifting and re-balancing our mind-body connections towards increased soothing, calm, and a sense of well-being.

The elation that arises from singing is from a release of endorphins or oxytocin, both associated with pleasure. In short, singing can be transformative. It is no surprise that singing is reported on the rise as it can literally and figuratively contribute to an overall harmonizing of people and environments. Group singing is no longer the domain of church choirs. There are many types of singing groups springing up throughout areas of work and community living.

"Singing Improves Health and Work Environment" (Science Nordic, Nov. 12. 2012) reported that employees in two hospitals in Norway decided on a project called, The Sound of Well-being, to see the impact of singing on its employees. There were two groups: employees that participated and those that did not. The overall finding was that those employees who participated in the singing groups reported a higher commitment to their workplace than their non-singing colleagues with an additional self-assessed improvement in their health over those who didn't participate.

CBC News (2015) reported an article on a music as medicine study that revealed classmates over a seven-month period at the University of Oxford's adult education courses bonded quickest through singing as compared to creative writing or crafts. The speed of the bonding pointed to a faster cohesion between unfamiliar individuals resulting in what researchers Pearce, Launay and Dunbar (2015) called the "ice-breaker effect of singing."

These kinds of positive vibrations extending out into our surrounding physical environment also have beneficial impact. For example, research being done by Dr. Monica Gagliano from the University of Western Australia sees plants as living dynamic sentient beings. She has extensively studied the relationship between plants and sound and she continuously hums and plays music to her plants.

Dr. Gagliano's work is prolific with countless publications that clearly demonstrate the intelligence of plant life and their ability to learn and interact with animals and humans. Her website, which addresses *"The Science of Plant Behaviour and Consciousness,"* is worth noting for a full range of her research publications: http://www.monicagagliano.com.

Drumming

As we still know it today, nearly every culture in the world has practiced some form of drumming. Shamans and healers worldwide have recognized drumming's holistic healing benefits. Drumming is also closely associated with First Nations peoples and some have referred to drumming as being the heartbeat of Mother Earth.

Drumming has been significantly used for healing, meditation, and for spiritual, social, political and civic ceremonies. It is recognized that drumming has been integral to music providing the backbone of the rhythm; the even metric beat that grounds the music and allows the creative instrumentals to flow.

Drumming as a stand-alone experience also has the same benefits that singing has but is more noteworthy for lowering blood pressure and stress through the act of hitting and hearing the beat. It can even become quickly meditative through repetition.

Drum circles are inclusive events for all-age groups that can involve just drumming or can also incorporate singing, body-percussion and guided imagery. Daniel Levitin, a McGill University researcher and co-author Monalisa Chandra (2013) acknowledged that, overall, music positively affects brain chemistry and mental health function by aiding in stress reduction, boosting immunity, managing mood, and assisting in social bonding. Most specifically, he cited that drumming circles for seniors also has the impact of reversing age-related deterioration.

In Vancouver, BC, facilitator, Lyle Povah, (2011), who researched a *Drum Circle Program for Eating Disorders at Saint Paul's Hospital,* purports that "in the health care environment, drum circles promote self-expression and self-empowerment. Following drum circles, patients report feeling more energized, relaxed and joyful."

In a well-known study by Dr. Barry Bittman (2001) the American neurologist introduced drumming in a Pennsylvania senior's nursing home over 6 weeks to research the benefits of drumming. He saw a 50% increase in staff mood and a decrease in depression and fatigue. He cited that "*group drumming tunes our biology, orchestrates our immunity, and enables healing to begin.*" (p. 38-47).

There has been a resurgence of drumming circles for all ages and across all societal areas including corporate arenas. On some of the local beaches around the British Columbia coasts for example, during the summer months you will hear the rhythmic, joyful, and enticing sounds of djembe and conga drums in the evenings that bring all ages together.

Using Color to Influence Energy

I consciously pick colors for my daily self-care to boost my energy, convey an impression, or simply help me feel emotionally comfortable. Color is important to us in where we live, and how we dress and feel. Colors also connect us.

An interesting phenomenon I've witnessed in workplaces is after several months of getting to know people, I've found three or four of us will turn up in exactly the same color on the same day. I've found that usually these colors reflect the colors of the upper chakras' emotional and spiritual colors of green, blue, violet or purple hues – making a simple demonstration of the closer emotional and spiritual link between us.

Color was widely recognized for centuries by the ancients and Indigenous peoples across continents for its importance in spiritual meaning, symbolism and ceremony. The use of colors encompasses many areas of our lives that continue to involve sacred and differing aspects in present diverse religions, spiritual beliefs, mood, as well as cultural and ceremonial practices and healings (Wills, 1993).

The colors that we wear, what we see in nature, and what we surround ourselves with in our homes and working environments, all act to influence us in body, mind, spirit as well as our behavior. Animals and plants are also affected by color, and each color also has its own vibration and measureable wavelength (Chambers, 2016).

When we begin with the natural light from the sun at dawn and continue through to the darkness of night after sunset, we are experiencing the powerful effects of the rainbow of colors contained in this electromagnetic spectrum of light from the sun. This light is akin to the same electromagnetic waves, like radio and television, and light is the natural part of the spectrum we can actually see. This natural light is made up of the primary colors of red, orange, yellow, green, blue, and violet.

We can see the primary colors when we allow light to flow through a prism and those colors fall into the rainbow pattern, or when we see a natural rainbow in the sky as light is dispersed and reflected through the droplets. On a practical level, we also use it to assess our degree of safety and determine what is alarming, threatening or pleasing to the eye in all situations and in all manner of food, plants, insects, animals, and people that come into our field of vision.

To consciously use color as an energy tool for self-care we can just first pay attention to what colors we are drawn to, as well as when and how we feel. Each color has its own energy vibration that has impact on us. Some colors will energize and invigorate us, soothe and calm us, or put us on alert. All colors have a dual psychological impression of negative and positive depending on what mood and situation we are in, and what message about ourselves we want to convey.

Traditionally, cross-culturally, spiritually, there can also be differences attributed to each color. For example, in western societies, black can symbolize formality and sophistication or dark and evil energy. In Egyptian culture, black can be associated with rebirth and transformation and, also in Africa, color can represent maturation, particularly for males (Wills, 1993, Wang, 2015). It's fascinating and useful to do some research on your own about the nature of color for different peoples.

Some colors included below will have similarities corresponding to chakra and auric colors. The list below reflects the main primary colors we tend to think of the most in western society.

Black: Black represents all colors absorbed into one and therefore there is an absence of light. Black can bring in a sense of authority, protection, glamour or sophistication. Conversely, it can also represent heaviness, coldness, a threat, or even oppression. If you are already feeling down, black may not be your best choice. If you choose to lighten it up, some of the more energetic colors below can help.

Brown: Brown is a natural, earthy color that represents reliability, groundedness, and warmth. Brown can also initially convey an impression of humbleness or sometimes of being too serious. This color can be helpful to soften, stabilize, and ground your energy.

Gray: Gray can be experienced as a kind of neutral color. It's not always best in exuding confidence unless you accent it with a brighter color, as it doesn't convey as much energy or vitality. Silver is actually gray with a metallic or polished sheen. This color can help to appear businesslike, but may lack a sense of warmth you might want to exude.

Red: Red is a strong color as it is most often connected to our physical senses, giving arousal to feelings of strength, passion and vitality. It can also awaken us to possible alarm, such as in the case of stop lights, police, or ambulance lights. Wear red to increase your energy and know that you will undoubtedly stand out. Red can also be interpreted as being a more assertive color. Some people can be intimated by wearing red and/or feel drawn to your vitality and self-confidence.

Pink: Pink is actually a tint derivative of red, but has a far more soothing effect on us, especially the pastel pinks, which are often seen as the more feminine, romantic, softer color against the more culturally active or masculinized color of red. Fortunately, our traditional, restrictive concepts of gender have become more human and expansive, and colors are also being used in a more expressive way, particularly by North American men.

Orange: Orange plays more into our sense of fun, comfort, warmth, and sensuality. It can assist to awaken our creativity. Orange is red and yellow combined. Some color specialists suggest that given the expansive nature of orange, it's good to combine it with a cooler color for balance such as blue.

Yellow: Yellow is seen as the strongest stimulating psychological color as its wavelength is long. One can experience optimism, emotional and intellectual strength, and extroversion when wearing or seeing this color. As with orange, a combined cooler color like blue or black is good for strength in balance. Gold is metallic yellow, or a yellow hue can also be referred to as golden.

Green: Green is a color whose impression is one of harmony, balance, love, healing, and peace. It is located in the center of the color spectrum and makes us feel closer to nature and all of her abundance. It can be calming and quietly energizing simultaneously, and it is often used in healing or medical centers to help people relax. Darker greens can impress as being wealthy. As an opposite impression, green can be seen as unmoving or even stagnate, or when associated with food – rancid.

Blue: Blue is perceived to be an intellectual color and gives rise to positive and efficient communication, calm, and coolness. Many people, including myself, will sometimes seek to wear blue near our throat chakra when wanting to ensure clear communications. Blue is often worn for job interviews, as it symbolizes loyalty. Contrasting impressions of blue can leave one feeling too cool, unemotional, unfeeling, or aloof.

Purple and/or Violet: These synonymous colors are most often connected to our sense of spirituality and spiritual awareness, truth, and inner vision. This color, depending on the hue, can both liven up your energy as well as create an impression of introversion and deeper thought.

White: White is the complete opposite of black and is a total reflection of all colors. It is often not so easy to look at white and is characterized as: pure, hygienic, simple, sophisticated, standoffish, and elite.

This information referenced in sum from:

Angela Wright, *Colour Affects*, 2008-1016; David, Johnson, Colour Psychology, *Do different colours affect your mood?* 2000-2016; Susana Martinex-Conde, Stephen L. Machknik, *How the Colour Red Influences Our Behaviour*. Scientific America, Behaviour and Society, 01.11, 2014); Pauline Wills, (1993) Colour Therapy, in Health Essentials, the use of Colour for Health and Healing.

Chapter 4
Protecting Your Energy

Protecting Your Energy Field

Protecting your energy field is about setting a boundary. As you set other kinds of emotional and physical boundaries, it's a good idea to also set a boundary around your entire auric field. Using your mental and visual capabilities is an important part of protecting yourself quickly on the unseen realm. Later on in this chapter we will also look at boundaries more closely connected to the emotional and physical body.

You can clear your auric field first by following the clearing exercises provided in chapter 3, or other exercises you prefer. You can also intend that the visualization below using white and violet light, also act as a clearing energy.

Exercise: The Egg and the Color of Violet

1. Focus on your breath and inhale a deep slow breath (count from 1 to 4) in through your nose and then out through your mouth (count from 1 to 4). Do this breathing three times.
2. Imagine pure white light descending from above your crown over your body and through your body down into the ground. Imagine it clearing out your auric field of unwanted negative thoughts or feelings – as well as from your inner chakras and any other cells of the body. Imagine it is now gently enwrapping you and covering your entire auric energy field like a giant egg, strong and protective in its very nature and shape. The egg shape is a loving symbol of Earth and of life.

3. When you have finished, and if you want to add an extra layer of protection, think about the color violet. Violet can be used as a protective color and an alchemic color of transmutation. I have used this color myself. It has origins that go back centuries with powerful connection to the ascended Master, Saint Germain.

4. Imagine this violet color now becomes a flame of violet color, gently flowing down through all your chakras and cells as well as over your entire auric field, covering the first protective egg shape you have created. The Violet Flame is another very powerful transmuter of negative energies. Besides shielding yourself, you can use it to shield animals, items, other people, and even places. You can command that this Violet Flame cleanse all negativity from your body, mind and spirit and protect your energy system.

The previous exercise is highly cursory, as I have used the formal invocations for the Violet Flame in my past meditative/spiritual practice. I will respectfully leave it for the reader, if interested, to acquire more understanding of this powerful realm and expansive use of the Violet Flame for protecting, transmuting, and healing energies. Some resources include:

- Prophet, E.C. (1997) *The Violet Flame to Heal Body, Mind and Soul*. Summit Publications, Inc.
- The Violet Flame (2016) *The Secret Of the Violet Flame* http://violetflame.com/violet-flame-secret/

Your Intention

The power of any of these protective measures lies in your clear and mindful intention to create them. We can all develop our own protective energy shields, because the power of our mental images, our words, and our beliefs are so strong as to be completely integral to our outer experiences being formed or co-created. What lies inside may eventually manifest outside.

I had my own protective shield shown to me as I was participating in a Reiki session. I felt and saw what appeared as a luminescent, multi-layered feathering covering of my entire auric field from head to toe. With practice, you will find your own image emerging for you that will become more meaningful and more powerful.

Invocations

There are other ways to give us protection. As in chapter 3, invoking the Angelic realm is a recognized way. Many people believe in the higher Angelic realm while others do not. Even if one does not believe in this spiritual realm, it does not mean angels do not exist. There are many documented stories about this powerful level of beings that defy normal human explanation.

There are now countless worldwide first-person reports of sudden encounters with strangers who appear out of nowhere and offer life-saving assistance, from unseen hands pulling people from disastrous situations to sudden warnings that prevent injuries or death.

One reference is *Proof of Angels* by Ptolemy Tompkins and Tyler Beddoes (2016) and another is John Geiger's book, *The Angel Effect* (2013). These authors have collected first-hand accounts from hundreds of offerings that tell of amazing and miraculous interventions. I have also experienced my own times of divine interventions that I strongly believe were the result of this higher realm stepping in with virtually no time to spare to intervene and save my life.

There are many other authors such as Doreen Virtue, Dianna Cooper, Lorna Byrne, and Dr. William Bloom, that have spent years giving detailed instruction and guidance as to how this powerful spiritual domain works including how each person's Guardian Angels can assist us daily in any area of our lives. As with any situation we are entering in advance, common sense always comes first in terms of routine and logical preparations.

If one wants to invoke the angelic realm in terms of acting in a greater protective manner, you can make this request of your Guardian Angels in any situation. Archangel Michael is also recognized to be the most powerful of the Archangels who will offer protection – emotionally, spiritually and physically. His attributes are: courage, strength, truth, and integrity. Simply ask mentally or verbally for Archangel Michael's assistance.

Ask for protection if you are going into any area that makes you feel vulnerable, or you feel you need an extra level of protection and support physically, emotionally or spiritually. Just ask and the Light Being will be there, whether that be your own personal Guardian Angel or an Archangel. Archangels have the ability to be in many places at one time because they are highly advanced multidimensional beings that are not restricted between worlds or dimensions of time and space, as we understand it.

Overall, another way of looking at this kind of request, if all of the above information seems beyond the scope of reality, is to simply consider the power of your own words. You may find an energetic thought forms as a request, prayer, or declaration. Your request is energetically powerful enough to invoke a manifestation of what you require.

The power of the spoken word cannot be underestimated, as it is a powerful command to the universal energy to co-create with you exactly what you are asking for (discussed in more detail in chapter 5). Ultimately, it is up to you and your comfort level because our personal beliefs hold power behind the request.

The Importance of Our Personal Boundaries

"The most important distinction anyone can ever make in their life is between who they are as an individual and their connection with others."

— **Anné Linden**

There are many different kinds of boundaries in our society. With regard to knowledge of our personal boundaries, very few of us in childhood are routinely taught the importance of knowing and asserting those core boundaries. If we have come from varying degrees of dysfunctional family backgrounds, then we often learn about our boundaries and our personal protective rights after they have been crossed.

Yet, boundaries are one of the most important things that define our identities and help keep us safe. Boundaries tell others what we value, what we believe in, how we choose to govern our lives, and how we want others to treat us. Essentially, there are four main boundary areas:

Physical Boundaries

Our physical boundaries, in terms of the degree of space in which we like to feel safe and comfortable, can be part of our cultural heritage as well as the nature of our friendships and intimate relationships. Other more obvious physical boundaries involve our personal spaces at home, at work, as well as our range of personal belongings as in my area and your area of material/boundary ownership.

An example of an important physical boundary revolves around touch. This is sometimes a confusing area for those who have been violated as children, as example, and have never been able to receive resolution to that violation. There are also those who may assume they are entitled to touch others as they wish without permission. Unwanted touching can reflect racism, sexism, and abuse of one's power and control. If you are not sure if someone has crossed this boundary with you, check in with yourself to see how you feel. If you experience a sense of being uncomfortable or recoil, then trust your feelings that your boundary was crossed.

Emotional Boundaries

Having a clear sense of how we feel about what is important to us, while at the same time being able to respectfully appreciate where someone else is at, even if we don't always agree, strikes a good balance for healthy emotional boundaries. Being able to disagree and assert our feelings and not cave into being manipulated (or manipulating others) is also part of healthy emotional boundaries.

If we feel taken for granted and there is a pattern evolving, that may be seen as having our emotional boundaries crossed. This is when our expressed needs and wants are ignored, or where we don't feel listened to or accepted for who we are. Respecting our own needs and wishes as being as valuable as those of others, and being able to state our own needs and wants clearly, is necessary for healthy, interdependent relationships.

Verbal name-calling, insults, or disrespectful language directed at you or anyone else is also a clear example of abuse of our emotional boundaries. Another aspect of emotional boundaries is how we can independently meet more of our own emotional needs without an inordinate reliance on someone else.

This move towards a greater sense of self as being whole and complete as we are helps strengthen us and deter our emotional attachments from becoming overly dependent, as in addictive or co-dependent relationships. Since the world we live in promotes addictions and over attachments every which way possible, this piece of gaining a greater independent whole and complete self can be a lengthier, evolving process.

Mental Boundaries

Mental boundaries are connected to how we value our personal thoughts and opinions and how we come to our own conclusions about how we live, what we value, and just about anything we choose to believe. When anyone tries to insert their opinions or thoughts into our mind frame, attempts to manipulate, control, or make us feel guilty or responsible for their behavior, then we are being signaled that our mental boundaries are being crossed. We can choose to assert our thoughts in respectful ways without intrusion.

Spiritual Boundaries

Our personal sense or views of what the Creator, God, Goddess, Allah, Buddha, Higher Self, ourselves as Divine, or anything else we name as a guiding force in our spiritual lives, is not for anyone else to determine or pressure us to acknowledge. If we do not believe in anything as being spiritually relevant to us, that is also acceptable. Spiritual boundary development can also involve those we agree to associate with who share similar thoughts, beliefs, feelings and views on life, as well as their personal conduct. It's an area of our overall discernment that requires a thoughtful approach.

Examples of Poor Boundaries
Too Open

Some peoples' boundaries are so open and flexible that their sense of limits feels practically non-existent. Unfortunately, this means that these kinds of open boundaries consciously and unconsciously grant others permission to behave in ways that can be disrespectful and take advantage of them, as there is nothing to hold them back. People who lack clear boundaries do no one any favors, especially themselves. The person's openness is not a bad thing, per se, but they need to honor and protect themselves appropriately.

Ambivalence

When our boundaries are not well defined, we can end up behaving in an ambivalent manner in not being able to make up our minds about what we want. This behavior only confuses and frustrates people. When people become confused about whom you are and what your intentions are, they have more difficultly knowing where they stand with you. Ambivalent behavior can create degrees of mistrust, sometimes even fear, and then, not surprisingly, disconnection. People inherently feel more secure with clear definitions.

Authoritative

The authoritative boundary person really does not want any discussion that challenges the limits and boundaries they have set. It's their way or the highway. This rigidness in boundary setting is often displayed in a kind of black-and-white thinking. The authoritative boundary person may voice ongoing blame and judgment without taking full responsibility for their own actions. Some people in parenting roles or in higher leadership positions within businesses, agencies, or corporate structures may tend to adopt this unfortunate style of boundary setting, thinking it shows strength when it actually shows the opposite, which is fear. This boundary expression can also be accompanied with the added confused message and double standard of do as I say, not as I do. When one continuously exhibits this style, others may show feelings of fear, mistrust, anger, leading to the boundary setter experiencing disconnection and isolation from people around them.

Good Boundaries Exude Strength

When you know what your boundaries are, people become instinctively aware of that fact because you will exude an unspoken strength. This strength acts as a deterrent to others who tend to practice control and manipulation. Your energy is not attractive to them. This strength also lets people know you are aware and respectful of their boundaries as well.

Good boundaries support and promote you to say no or yes in various circumstances that require you to regulate all manner of people, situations and demands that enter your life. Unregulated demands and stresses can become overwhelming. We see evidence of this in people who are over extended, leading to staff burnout in most of the social service and health care arenas. This energy exhaustion and burnout can occur from the front line, to middle management, and up the director's level.

The ability to consciously regulate the stimuli in your personal as well as your daily work-life will also allow you to feel more confident to express yourself in a more authentic way. Your realness will pull in more of the respect you deserve. You will also attract better personal and work-life circumstances because respecting yourself draws respect from others. We are constantly teaching people how to treat us.

If you've not practiced being definitive before, defining and standing up for your boundaries in personal relationships will bring challenges from family, friends, or even ex-partners. It can surprise anyone who may have enjoyed receiving your services or attention in a manner that no longer serves you. In short, they probably won't be too happy about your stand for clarity and limit setting, and you may ultimately receive comments to suggest your attitude needs a serious adjustment. Just stand firm in your decision to support your true worth and uphold what you most treasure – yourself.

Know Yourself

Knowing yourself is about setting boundaries around your time and how to balance between your responsibilities as a parent, caregiver and/or wage earner, and your need for personal time-out and self-care. Often these are just not easy decisions to make.

We sometimes do not have clarity about ourselves over the course of a hectic or chaotic day, and in those moments, you will need to take time to go inward, take a few breaths, and reflect on how you really feel to re-establish some clarity around your time and space. In those moments, just remember to sit quietly and breathe in and out. This will immediately begin to quiet your mind for clearer inner listening. You can use any of the grounding, clearing and protection measures you've read.

The clarity that comes from practice in focusing on your feelings, wishes, and nourishment needs is important to setting good boundaries. It is also good to have a sense of your own pace regarding how fast or slow you like to do things. If someone is making a request of your time and you are not sure about that request, establish for yourself how much time you have left in a day – automatically include a few moments for yourself – then pace more slowly in terms of what kind of time is actually realistic for you to give, and in what manner and context.

Setting Boundaries

Setting boundaries means clarifying and making mindful, informed decisions:

What it is you really want to do?
When is the best time and date for you?
With whom are you really willing to invest your time?
How much mental, physical, emotional, financial energy are you willing to expend to the situation?
Where will you be, and is the environment safe? Does it work positively for you in terms of noise or crowdedness?

Knowing the above will allow you to:

- Clearly know and speak your limits to those around you

- Support your words with an appropriate decision that bolsters your well-being
- Maintain consistency in your responses
- Teach others how to respect and treat you

If you feel indecisive that usually indicates a lack of information about any of the above questions. It may also mean the timing for you to participate may not be right.

Saying No and Feelings of Guilt

If you set a boundary and feel guilty, that's not a bad sign. It generally means you are re-setting the expectations of yourself and others that may have kept you in place and even entrapped. It's an emotional adjustment process and it takes time and patience.

Setting personal boundaries and sticking to them amidst others complaints that their needs are not being met can initially feel selfish or self-centered, but it's really about honoring and respecting yourself. People don't often like change when they experience you as taking yourself away from meeting their needs or abandoning them. However, they'll have to get used to the new you and adjust themselves accordingly. This is where co-dependent or simply unhealthy, unbalanced relationships show up.

You may realize you have been an over-functioning participant, as many of us are for periods of time. Moving away from these over-functioning, caregiving, or rescuing roles will bring you more vitality and focus to accomplish more of what matters to you.

Your life's mission and passions will also reveal themselves more clearly to you. You will have successfully made emotional and psychological room for them to be heard from within. Some boundaries may need to be non-negotiable resulting in a strict do-not-cross boundary setting. Overall, it's important to know what boundaries are so important for you to safeguard that they are not to be tampered with at any cost.

Assertiveness Exercise

This exercise is meant to help you get started in a process of thinking assertively to draw in more strength from any measure of past success. Thinking about self-assertion is the first step in getting your frame of mind to back you up, followed by seeking out more help, if necessary, towards taking action to accomplish your goal.

- Think of a time in your life that you felt the strongest in terms of following a path that you knew was clearly right for you. You can be any adult age (or even a child). Think of your deep commitment to following your plan through. How did you accomplish your goal? Who was there, or what was in place to assist you?
- Think of any measure of happiness, sense of pride, or any degree of accomplishment that you experienced along the way. See if you can also recall somewhere inside yourself when you said no to whomever or whatever might potentially stand in the way of your success. Feel again your commitment to stand your ground and move yourself forward.
- Think of a present situation that is bothering you, or a habit you want to be free of that is not supporting your health. Draw up your past memory and allow the strength that you had inside of you then to come forward into this present situation. Really get into the mind-set of yourself in that past time and your commitment to succeed.
- Stay in that mind-set and write down any words that come to you about how you felt. Know that as soon as you put your mind in that same frame from your past, you are already on the right track to accomplishing this goal.
- Picture yourself standing strong in your commitment to assert yourself. See yourself stepping back or away from the current situation or negative behavior habit.

Assertive Bill of Rights

Gael Lindenfield is recognized as a leading personal development trainer in the United Kingdom and has listed the following assertive rights. This list can be a helpful reminder to carry with you, or to keep in an easy place to see.

- The right to ask for what we want, realizing that the other person has the right to say no.
- The right to have an opinion, feelings, and emotions and to express them appropriately.
- The right to make statements which have no logical basis and which we do not have to justify.
- The right to make our own decisions and to cope with the consequences.
- The right to choose whether or not to get involved with the problems of someone else.
- The right to know about something, or to understand.
- The right to make mistakes.
- The right to be successful.
- The right to change our mind.
- The right to privacy.
- The right to be alone and independent.
- The right to change ourselves and be assertive people.

http://www.londonstressmanagement.com/client_download s/Assertive%20Bill%20of%20Rights.pdf

"Would I allow my inner child into this situation?"

This question can be used by anyone to bring forward any feelings that might intuit if a situation is safe or unsafe. It is a very useful question for those are familiar with the concept of their inner child, a term used in aspects of psychological healing work to bring us back to the wisdom or playfulness of our younger self. We can also experience our inner child when we are more frightened or vulnerable in situations. She or he will give us a gut sense or intuitive messages about what is safe, or is not safe or comfortable for us. His or her feelings are worth listening to.

To get in touch with your inner child, picture yourself as you were when you were about eight years or so. Now you, in your adult state, are the protective parent of your younger you who stands before you. You agree that you will always take care of your inner child, as best as you can, and will not force her or him into unsafe or unhealthy situations. Your responsibility is to always try to make the right decision on behalf of this child. This includes always checking in to listen to him or her as to how he or she is feeling, particularly in moments of stress, anxiety, fear, or uncertainty. Hug your little kid and tell her or him, "I am here for you now and I love you."

Recommended References:

- *Better Boundaries, Owning and Treasuring Your Life,* by Jan Black and Greg Enns, (1997)
- *"Building Better Boundaries"* by The Self Help Alliance, University of Alberta, as a good worksheet for boundary recognition and strengthening. (Terms for use cited). PDF website: Building Better Boundaries. https://www.ualberta.ca/medicine/departments/anethes ology-pain-medicine/staff-well-being/

In sum, when you choose to assert limits and boundaries to protect and support yourself in nourishing ways, your self-regard will also help others around you. Although there can be times when you are met be with resistance to your changes, your self-strengthening can encourage the potential within everyone connected to you, to recognize the necessity to strengthen their abilities to meet their own needs.

Chapter 5
Mindful Communication Part 1

"Mind is a flexible mirror, adjust it, to see a better world."
– Amit Ray

The Conscious Mind

To fully care for ourselves we need to also care for our minds in understanding what affects our mental states positively or otherwise. Generally, mindfulness is about being aware and objective of what is going on in our thoughts and feelings in various moments without judgment or criticism. In this mindful objectivity, we can further cultivate a consciousness to accept ourselves with compassion in the full range of our humanness, appreciating that we are all learning and evolving on our own personal paths.

Becoming more mindful is not always easy to do as there are countless daily distractions. It takes practice and vigilance over a life-time. Becoming more consciously aware and mindful will contribute to taking far more control over our thoughts and feelings and it will contribute to being more peaceful and balanced in all our energy systems. This increased inner peace and balance will be reflected in experiencing the world in more peaceful ways.

Before many of us can get to the kind of "Zen-like" state we'd like, there can be moments where it seems we are at the mercy of our thoughts – and that's unpleasant if those thoughts are more negative or fearful. Being immediately aware of the influences behind those kinds of thought patterns will also help us know how we might be communicating our inner experiences to others - and then making changes as necessary towards more peaceful interactions.

Default to the Negative

Though most people want to remain positive and hopeful, we do have a human tendency to default to the negative – where we can quickly assume the worst in people or see situations most often from a fearful, negative standpoint. Defaulting to the negative is not to cast blame on ourselves for this learned habit of thinking. We can all fall into this tendency easily when we hear ourselves jumping to conclusions and, if there is something positive to consider, we ignore or invalidate it.

This tendency can also be rooted in past hurts or traumas that emerge when triggered by a comment from someone that reminds us of that negative time. Listening to our self-talk can give us a clue as to how quickly we turn to perceive situations in a pessimistic light, or if we are able to step back and think more critically to see a fuller picture.

Some researchers think this default tendency towards mistrust, worry or gloom is a hardwired evolutionary pattern for our brains as a result of past survival issues meant to keep us alert. It is often referred to as our reptilian brain. The reptilian brain is the part of our brain that is shared by the animals on our planet and it involves instinctual triggers leading to fear and fight-or-flight reactions. The reptilian brain also creates the need to want to group together – to feel safer and stronger for maximum protection – with a focus on defending our perceived territory.

At present, with the increase in the socio-political, economic, and environmental changes occurring on a global level, there is greater instability being experienced en masse and it is triggering a resurgence of our reptilian brain.

That being said, there are a lot of sad and frightening things going on in this world that are continuously influencing our collective perceptions to the negative. Our thoughts, unless consciously trained to the contrary, can make us vulnerable to be drawn in to pay even closer attention to the psychologically darker, weightier information that crosses our path.

What we can do instead is try to choose to be aware of this easy default tendency and watch incoming information with discernment. We can then cultivate our minds towards more balanced, solution-focused, and uplifting thoughts without completely denying the difficult realities occurring on this planet. We can choose to open other doors to more hope, love, and kindness.

Media Watch

We have some excellent journalistic reporting as well as thoughtful and informative programming to available for us to choose from on a global level. We have our favorite sports, comedies, reality TV, dramas and everything else in between. Having more programming also means there is more news and likely more violence to sift through.

Negative thoughts coming in produce negative thoughts going out. Mainstream and alternative media outlets are aware of how populations tend towards drama, fear, and gossip. Media also includes all manner of information streaming on the Internet. All of this communication continues to systemically impact us with overt and subliminal messages. Images and themes in movies, TV news, social-tabloid magazines, and digital games, all have the power to shape our perceptions, affect our feelings and can even result in having a depressing physical effect on us if its content is mostly slanted in one negative direction.

It's truly dreadful to know about the suffering and abuse in our world through war and other forms of death that bring despair. The onslaught of images and information on a daily basis begins to create a powerful impression that our world is primarily a wholly negative and unsafe place to be. Perhaps we can say with a degree of certainty that some kinds of information and images being disseminated from various outlets can become remarkably addictive as in a type of fear porn as we, the general public, becomes increasingly emotionally desensitized to violence and images of death. As this desensitization continues, we are pulled away from our gentle heartedness and we risk leaving behind our inner sense that tells us something isn't right about all of this.

We are also seeing the advent of more fake news. Becoming more individually critically attentive seems to be the call concerning the quality of journalism and the kind of media messages we're exposed to. I spoke recently to a student well versed in journalism studies and she voiced her concerns about the erosion of the quality and quantity of our local community-based news; news that provides core substance material and is integral to our national coverage.

The importance of maintaining high quality, balanced, and credible journalism coverage to remain in place locally, regionally, and nationally now is one to watch for. Balanced reporting is vital to let us know what is going on in the world, such as amazing innovative or restorative contributions people are making in so many areas, accomplishments on behalf of the planet, people, and animals, lifesaving moments, medical healing miracles, stories of caring and kindness between people, and the way we support and help restore one another.

There is a simple, albeit partial, solution: turn off the TV more often. If we can look at stepping back from some of this low-frequency energy programming and take a little more time to uplift ourselves through reading, taking up a hobby, walking out in nature, or getting into some kind of exercise routine, it can definitely help.

Positive activities might be considered a form of distraction, but they can also be a way to care about our minds and how we are choosing to allow negative or positive information to influence us. Turning off the fear can help reduce some of our world's extreme, heavy-weighted news and other dramas that promote even more fear, stress, and anxiety through those specific portals.

Communication in Stressful Situations

We know stress, positive or negative, is part of life, but too much stress creates a constriction in our mind-spirit-body and our vitality diminishes. As this lowering of our energy increases, our perceptions of what is actually occurring around us also becomes more limited.

Again, we begin to default to the negative as we develop tunnel vision, become judgmental and inaccurate in our assessments about one another's intentions and actions. We often don't hear what is actually being communicated and we can misconstrue messages through an increasingly negative filter. Our communication can become less than hospitable and we can start blaming others.

Horizontal hostility is a term used to describe hostile and blaming communication between coworkers within a workplace, who may unconsciously begin to adopt a superior view of other staff. This attitudinal shift can happen for a variety of reasons but notably when people aren't aware or able to openly express their stresses and frustrations to the governing powers that be.

The term horizontal hostility originated from the feminist movement in the 1970s to describe discord, infighting, and fractionalization between members of subgroups, rather than banding together to promote collation building to advance their cause (White and Langer, 1999).

Horizontal hostility has since become a generalized term to refer to behavior and dynamics of power, control, and dominance, aka lateral violence, between workmates that resemble the very behaviors they usually normally, morally, and ethically oppose (London Health Sciences Centre, 2009).

This kind of hostility being transferred to others can happen anywhere when we are in a state of holding in, accumulating excess stress, fear, anxieties, or frustrations and do not have a positive outlet to express what's happening for us. These emotions can build up and we unfortunately and unintentionally can find ourselves getting triggered and dishing it out to some degree to our loved ones and friends if we have lost some measure of our mindfulness about what is going on inside.

The Ease and Divisiveness of Gossip

Don Miguel Ruiz, author of the 1997 book *The Four Agreements: A Practical Guide to Personal Freedom*, emphasizes the power of the spoken word as a "gift from God" – an essential tool in humanity's code of mindful conduct. With the right use of our words, we can either dishearten people, or encourage and inspire them. We have the ability to use our words to help create healing situations and extend caring and compassion to each other. When we do this, we should know that our caring energy ripples out and extends beyond everyone we give support to.

As people are naturally curious about each other we like to positively share our own and others' interests, experiences and accomplishments. However, there is a negative downside to our sharing. We are familiar with the term "office gossip" or gossip that occurs anywhere.

The Oxford English dictionary defines gossip, once known as tattletales, as "casual or unconstrained conversation or reports about other people, typically involving details which are not confirmed as true." Knowing the difference between whether we are engaging in a natural, caring, and curious conversation or participating in degree of hostility challenges our intention about the information we are sharing.

Gossip can often signal there are communication difficulties between colleagues, or management and staff, where there is fear or lack of skill about how to speak to one another safely and openly to resolve issues. Comments based on assumptions and perceptual distortions do not add to a positive tone in an organization, and can happen more often when there are high levels of stress and a lack of positive outlets.

In 2015, Vancouver Coastal Health (VCH) a progressive health agency was one of the first employers in Canada to actively address elements involved in disrespectful behavior, of which gossip is an element cited. VCH created a confidential 1-800 line to report unresolvable disrespectful behavior and concomitantly offer support for staff and managers for resolutions. (http://www.vch.ca/media/VCH-anti-bullying-open-board-feb-2105.pdf)

Gossip is actually very common in human communication and similarly within much of the entertainment media. There is always a potential for misinformation. The following simple questions originating from Socrates can be helpful to consciously remind us of our intentions in our communication:

- Is it true?
- Is it kind?
- Is it necessary?

Our relationships can go more smoothly when we keep the intent of our communication as clear as possible and when we are able to deal quickly if there are signs of tension, confusion, misinformation or discord.

Vibrational Levels of Emotions

The stresses we experience from many sudden external sources, events and incidents, combined with our own inner issues and feelings, pose challenging emotional states. We can experience degrees of emotional ups and downs in our energy levels during the course of a day.

David Hawkins, MD. Ph. D. explains in *Power vs. Force: The Hidden Determinations of Human Behaviour* (2012), how our emotional states can pivotally influence our vibrational frequencies and, ultimately, how we move from a higher vibrational energy to a much lower one. Having an ongoing sense as to how we are feeling and what is affecting us is foundational to our self-care. We can operate in various kinds of emotional states depending on which environment we are in at the time, who we are interacting with, how physically well we feel at the time, and many other interrelating factors. Hawkins describes an individual's overall level of consciousness "is the sum of the total effect of all these various levels" (p. 97-98).

Hawkins' frequency levels shows that when we are involved in feelings of shame, guilt, apathy, and grief, we are actually in such a low-energy level that it is similar to when we are entering a state of overall demise. When we are feeling fear, anger, desire, and pride our vibrational level becomes more elevated from that lowered state. Finally, when we reach into the emotion of inner courage we allow for more life force to flow through us. We do feel better and far more energized. From that level of courage, we can move onward toward the most resilient and highest vibrational levels of love, joy, and enlightenment.

I relate to Hawkins' information to varying degrees, particularly in times of significant life losses. The amount of energy I've had in these times has been decisively lower as I move through a grieving process. Grieving and loss states can have us feeling like we are moving through a dense fog or even physically like we are so low in our energy as to be almost walking through mud. As well, we can understand if we've ever had to work through any experiences of shame or guilt as described below, in those times one's energy can plummet.

Level 20: Shame
Painful feeling of humiliation, distress, and whole person devaluing.

Level 30: Guilt
Feeling culpable for mistake or offence in behavior, emotional manipulation.

Level 50: Apathy
Indifference, lack of concern, lethargy, passivity, lack of responsiveness.

Level 75: Grief
Sorrow, dejection, despair, misery, anguish, deeply burdened.

Level 100: Fear
Fright, terror, agitation, alarm, anxiety, feeling under threat, immobilized.

Level 125: Desire
Wanting or wishing for something not received. Can experience as a lacking.

Level 150: Anger
Annoyance, exasperation, hostility, indignation, irritability, and vengeance.

Level 175: Pride
A rise in self-esteem but the ego is vulnerable to external opinions, which can fluctuate and send the vibration upward, or downward to superiority.

Level 200: Courage

Strength or valor shown in the face of fear, terror, and grief.

Level 250: Neutrality
Ability to hold a peaceful emotionally neutral, no-sides vantage point, higher observations.

Level 320: Willingness
Readiness to engage or assist in the moment. Can be inspirational.

Level 350: Acceptance
Receiving a person or a situation in openness and acceptable as is. Expansion of perception.

Level 400: Reason
The ability to use the mind to integrate and present a wide variety of information for understanding with emotional objectivity.

Level 500: Love
A higher conscious experience of Love as unconditional, void of attachment to outcomes, fear or dependency on another. Loving above and through discord.

Level 540: Joy
Expansion of the unconditional aspect of Love, such as patience and positivity. Notably hallmarked by compassion. A sense of lightness that arises from within, leading to inner joy and healing.

Level 600: Peace
A state that experiences transcendence, bliss and self-realization; dissolution of religious affiliations; has acquired abiding awareness of the sacred energy or Presence in all matter, aka God consciousness.

Level 700-1000: Enlightenment

The level of the non-duality and spiritually self-transcended Divine Masters or Avatars in our history such as Lord Krishna, Lord Buddha, Lord window (aka, Lord Sananda), Swami Vivekanada and Count Saint Germain, as a few, who mastered complete Oneness and Divine Grace with all.

All of these levels, as they move from lower to highest vibrations can help us appreciate our lack of energy when we have experienced emotional injury, are feeling down in the dumps, or when we are in state of stress, fear, or anger. For many of us, these emotional states are situational and fluctuating. For others, they can remain static for longer periods of time.

For everyone, our vibrational energy levels will fluctuate continuously and more acutely the more unexpected changes occur in our lives and bring more uncertainty. Hawkins' emotional vibrational states are worth keeping in mind as we look at what emotional energetic states lift or lower our energies. As energy moves and is contagious, one or several people in an organization will eventually impact the site as a whole, if they are routinely energizing to the positive or defaulting to the negative.

With so many changes underway across every spectrum in our world, new and innovative opportunities are being created to advance us forward. However, within the daily work world many of these opportunities for change have increased employee stress levels and brought on change fatigue. Changes occurring so swiftly and concurrently are testing our personal and collective resilience.

In addition to stresses from ongoing organizational changes, other stress symptoms can occur simultaneously, particularly from within the social service, health care or other related helping occupations where staff deal more directly with client trauma, illness, and abuse. The nature of these stresses can result in what is known as compassion fatigue.

This type of fatigue can occur simultaneously with change fatigue. This situation can happen particularly if you work in one of the helping organizations also involved with ongoing multiple change initiatives. We will discuss that change/compassion fatigue intersection later on in this chapter. First, we will look at the issue of change fatigue and its symptoms.

Change Fatigue

We know change is a fact of life and our ability to withstand, adapt, and transition forward with changes has become more important than ever. Globalization, technology, automation, and business competition are some of the elements driving many of our local, regional and national change initiatives.

I am someone who generally doesn't mind change as it gives me energy in its variety and continuous learning. However, too much change for too long without a period of reprieve or time-out is stressful and unpleasant. Too much change, too soon in an unplanned way can negatively impact small or larger organizations.

In my experience in social work positions at different agencies over many years I've had the opportunity to work primarily with managers and leaders who have taken time to try to plan change initiatives that included receiving input from staff and providing support for staff and clients. We know much more about change management processes now than in past years and we are still learning as we go.

Change does seem to be occurring more rapidly than ever now and there is growing concern that change has become too common within some organizations. More staff are responding that they do not have the ability or the necessary energy to fully carry through on these initiations.

Frontline and middle management employees are showing their weariness through passive resistance responses or a general sense of apathy and disengagement, rather than actual conscious refusal to participate (Turner, 2015; Morgan, 2001). This resistance can suggest that a point of personal saturation is being reached if initiations have been occurring rapidly and there is no stabilization in-between time before the next change is brought in.

In his 2009 book *Managing Transitions: Making the Most of Change*. author William Bridges writes:

"We talk not of a single change but of change as an ongoing phenomenon. It is collage, not a simple image: one change overlaps with another, and it's all change as far as the eye can see." (p. 99)

Bridges details the complexities and difficulties for people dealing with ongoing change and states that it isn't so much the pace of the change as the increased acceleration of the pace. As a result of not being able to acclimatize to the waves of change rushing in, the result is that we are thrown into transitions. Each transition in itself, accompanying each level of change is another process that involves three phases, namely:

1. **An ending, letting go, losses** of the old process are expressed.
2. **A neutral zone,** where there is a confused, in-limbo effect; an uncomfortable state of fluidity in not yet established in new processes or procedures.
3. **A new beginning** with ambivalence, fears, complaints, kudos, and innovations with an eventual go forward.

These phases do not have clearly defined boundaries, and if there are multiple changes occurring at once, the overflowing cauldron of transitional shifts can stretch the most resilient individual's ability to embrace changes without suffering fatigue.

We each have different ways of coping and adapting to change and some of us are more resilient than others due to various factors. Overall, change fatigue can be described as the amount of changes occurring being beyond an employee's capacity to effectively manage the changes. When change fatigue is left unattended, it can lead to degrees of burnout that is characterized by emotional exhaustion, powerlessness, and low job satisfaction.

Change Fatigue Symptoms:

- Disengagement, apathy, and indifference
- Mental and emotional fatigue
- Anxiety, stress, and weariness

- Confusion
- More complaints, and noise from employees
- Cynicism and skepticism
- Burnout

(Prosci: *5 Tips for: Addressing Change Saturation. Change Management Tutorial. (1996-2014)*
http://www.change-management.com/tutorial-5-tips-saturation).

Turner (2015) purports that change fatigue can also be experienced on a continuum. From the onset, employees can feel apathy and disengagement. Unless these initial symptoms are recognized and addressed they can progress with further negative impact on employees' productivity and their organization's loss in revenue – with the possible outcome of the change initiative failing.

Jeannie Duck (1993) cites in an article *Managing the Change: The Art of Balancing,* that within a continuum of constant change there are also "change survivors". These are employees that have been through so many ongoing change initiatives that they have perfected a measured way of behavior. This behavior is really an adapted coping in that they appear to be involved in the change initiative enough to survive it, yet do not fully perform the changes requested.

While on some level, this adaptive skill is notable and understandable, when left unrecognized; it can allow cynicism, a lack of productivity, and even compromise to client service to continue on. While these issues are occurring an attitude and practice of "just getting through the day" goes on. (Harvard Business Review: https://hbr.org/1993/11/managing-change-the-art-of-balancing, November-December Issue, 1993. par. 24).

Change Fatigue Factors

Periods of transitions and specific changes can naturally bring a measure of fatigue and stress during the overall change process. There are a number of factors that contribute to change fatigue and they can include:

- The magnitude of the perceived change
- Employees perceived need of the change
- How adept the organization is at change management processes to provide adequate supports for staff
- Unanticipated impact on other groups or parts of an organization when one initiation is being managed
- Whether or not a change was actually anticipated; what other changes are occurring at the same time of the newest change initiative
- The degrees of disruption experienced in the work and, as a consequence, upon personal lives, as a result of the initiated change (e.g. increased requests for overtime to accomplish workload).

(Turner, 2015; Prosci, 1996-2014)

Change Initiations and Caring for Staff

Prosci notes that it is critical that for change to work it must be managed well from a people perspective that takes into account any cumulative and collective impact on staff, as well as the points of systemic collision with any proposed solutions.

Prosci also acknowledges regarding "change saturation" that there is simply a limited capacity for ongoing change in any organization. http://www.change-management.com/tutorial-saturation-white-paper.htm (1996-2014, par. 4).

Turner (2015) adds insight by stressing that even smaller changes that are offered to organizations as non-project based changes must also practice change management processes. These perceptually smaller changes or systemic tweaks in our systems that are inherently added onto the side of the desk, over time create a cumulative degree of employee stress, overwhelm, frustration and disengagement leading once again to change fatigue.

Additionally, when managers do recognize employee symptoms of change fatigue they need to prepare to openly and supportively address them individually and, if necessary, collectively within the larger organizational structure. Moreover, management may need to take action to further re-prioritize change initiatives. This can be done by slowing down or even suspending initiatives until a more restful period takes place for staff's psychological and emotional stabilization and integration of any recent or ongoing organizational changes.

Although it might seem counterproductive, unnecessary and simply too time-consuming, change management elements that are used for bigger change initiatives should also apply to other smaller changes as well.

Henry Hornstein, Assistant Professor at the Ivey Business School (2008) reports that there are now more information technology changes occurring in all sectors of business and services that can potentially threaten staff when there is a lack of information and meaningful processes implemented.

Therefore, management and leadership's mindfulness in keeping the human factor in mind is critical. This mindfulness in sound change management processes can help in significantly assuaging potential health concerns brought on by challenging changes. Hornstein goes on to cite his recommended change management approaches:

- **Participatory Leadership**: honoring the values that allow for fullest collaboration between staff and leadership
- **Empowerment:** including staff input in initiatives; appropriately sharing decision-making responsibilities between management, leaders and staff
- **Systems thinking:** ability to anticipate the unexpected within the system upon change initiation

In conjunction with the above processes, 8 elements are considered foundational for successful change management as offered below, by John P. Kotter, Konosuke Matsushita Professor of Leadership, Emeritus at the Harvard Business School (2008).

These elements are capsulated below and essentially recognize the need for mindful communication between management, leadership, and staff and the respectful engagement of all employees in the change process:

- Establishing the urgency of why specific change opportunities need accomplishment now
- Creating a cohesive working group to lead the change initiative
- Creating a realistic vision and strategies for achievement
- Consistent and timely communication of progress of strategies with role modelling for staff's expected behaviors.
- Encouraging all employees to offer the leadership working group their creative input as to what is and what is not working in any of the change strategies
- Generating short-term wins with visible employee recognition
- Recognizing any polices, systems and structures that are outdated and creating new employee opportunities to move the enhanced vision forward throughout the organization
- Seeking to improve and culturally anchor organizational change through client/customer feedback that informs leadership and employees of successes while concomitantly offering leadership and employee development and succession

https://www.alaska.edu/files/pres/Leading-Change.pdf (p. 4)

Progressive change management practices that are meaningful and relevant to staff and client needs are believed to save time and build employee and management's capacity to handle changes better. These practices foster stronger bonds of trust between managers, leaders, and staff – and ultimately benefits clients and customers.

By practicing change management processes with sensitivity and awareness as to what staff are already experiencing, it will encourage staff to be more willing to participate. It will also allow integration of new information and change processes in a timelier manner. This style of consistent change management approach will also avoid the duplication of previous change initiatives. Managers will be far less likely to hear their staff say, "We did this same initiative two years ago. It didn't work then and it won't work now", or "What did they do with all that information from those other initiatives?"

Since change is arriving at a faster pace than a decade ago, practicing fuller scope change management procedures can allow an organization to become more resilient and change-ready. Progressive change management can also bring awareness and encouragement towards staff and managers' self-care and work/life balance practices when moving through change processes.

With these change management considerations in mind, we turn our attention in the next chapter to compassion fatigue and vicarious trauma being experienced primarily within the helping/caregiving arenas, and see that these occupations also have strong potential to intersect with change fatigue factors. This intersection emphasizes a great need for personal and organizational strategies for self-care.

Chapter 6
Mindful Communication – Part 2

Compassion Fatigue and Vicarious Trauma

Although this chapter has a greater emphasis on health care, social service workers and emergency responders, many of us can still be affected by compassion fatigue, vicarious trauma or even post-traumatic stress symptoms regardless of our occupation.

For example, if we are in the significant role as caregiver to a family member or if we know of a war veteran or refugee who has suffered from their experiences, or if we ourselves have ever experienced a distressing, traumatic event, then the information presented in this chapter can also provide helpful and compassionate insights for us all.

Being empathetic, caring, and open hearted are some of the very reasons why many people in the helping professions are vulnerable to feeling compassion fatigue and why there is a strong need to attend to their self-care.

The changing world is allowing us to become more knowledgeable of the experiences of many immigrants and refugees and their stories of catastrophe, horror, torture and traumatic losses. There are also more sexual abuse survivors and Indigenous Peoples coming forward to disclose painful incidents of life long violations. Increasing numbers of veterans also need much support and healing from the long-term effects of war's brutality.

Many of us in any of the helping occupations have also experienced trauma in our own lives. Even when we have made efforts to heal from them, there is still a good chance we will be more vulnerable to secondary or vicarious trauma and the varied stress-related symptoms especially when providing care to others who are still experiencing their trauma.

Having the insights born of our own traumas can become a gift to guide ourselves and others in time, but one in which we still need to be aware of our potential vulnerability and continued need for good self-care.

There is a great deal of material that's now been amassed about compassion fatigue and vicarious trauma in the past years. The following are the key points from the work and research of many practitioners and authors in this field.

Compassion Fatigue (CF) has often been used interchangeably with the term vicarious trauma and while they are interrelated, they can also be different. In viewing this conjoint relationship, the Traumatology Institute in Toronto, Ontario, suggests that compassion fatigue is an occupational hazard for those working most frequently with trauma sufferers.

These people would most typically be police officers, nurses, doctors, social workers, counsellors, paramedics, and personal health care givers. This information would also include family caring for their elderly family members, although there are other issues more specific to this group that I will address separately below.

These caregivers, helpers, or professional responders are particularly vulnerable and at risk to experience compassion fatigue from their work if symptoms are left unrecognized and unmanaged. Since empathy and compassion are the very attributes that bring these people into the helping professions, we can assume that anyone who cares about their clients or patients, or is in a caregiving capacity with their loved ones for extended periods of time, can be at risk for experiencing compassion fatigue to varying degrees.

Vicarious Trauma (VT) is not a signal that we are weak or unable to remain in our professions. It is a normal response and can be experienced as part of the continuum of severity of compassion fatigue where the service provider can begin to experience their own worldview shifting to such an extent that they develop similar, secondary, or vicarious traumatic stress symptoms as those who have suffered the event directly (Gangsei, D., 2011).

The experience of vicarious trauma can also stem from witnessing a one-time traumatic event. If the experience is so traumatic for the witness, the caregiver may also develop Post-Traumatic Stress Disorder (PTSD) symptoms more relative to the specific traumatic event.

For larger events, compassion fatigue, vicarious trauma with possible attending PTSD is also found for responders at scenes of community disasters of floods, fire, earthquakes, motor vehicle accidents, or flight crashes, as well as for various responders assisting people in war zones. Even the recent massive scale of refugees fleeing to settlements across Europe and other parts of the globe has resulted in an overwhelming amount of CV, VT, and PTSD for those trying to assist in ongoing refugee settlement efforts. (*Europe's Compassion Fatigue, 2015.* theAustralian.com.au)

Symptoms of Compassion Fatigue and Vicarious Trauma

- Emotional and mental exhaustion
- Diminished ability to feel empathy or compassion; insensitivity
- Reduced enjoyment of previous activities
- Lack of clarity in decision making
- Irritability, anger and sometimes rage
- Hypersensitivity or insensitivity to emotional material
- Susceptibility to illness/absenteeism
- Avoidance or dread of working with specific clients
- Decreased interest in maintaining quality client care
- Increased use of alcohol or other mood-altering substances
- PTSD symptoms (associated with vicarious trauma)

    o Flashbacks of traumatic event
    o Difficulty sleeping
    o Emotional liability
    o Numbness, flatness or emotional detachment
    o Nightmares

(Mathieu, F. (2007) Running on Empty: Compassion fatigue in Health Professional

http://www.compassionfatigue.org/pages/RunningOnEmpty.pdf;

Meichenbaum, D. & Research Director of The Melissa Institute for Violence Prevention and Treatment of Victims of Violence Miami, Florida, SELF-CARE FOR TRAUMA PSYCHOTHERAPISTS AND CAREGIVERS: INDIVIDUAL, SOCIAL AND ORGANIZATIONAL INTERVENTIONS.

https://www.melissainstitute.org/documents/Meichenbaum_SelfCare_11thconf.pdf CIAL)

Compassion Fatigue and Vicarious Trauma Factors

CF and VT have symptoms and factors have become more familiar to me as a social worker and in working with many trauma survivors to whom I have been able to give services to. The reasons for CF and VT have been provided in part in the previous discussion as to who is more vulnerable to experience CF and VT. Below is a capsulation of some common CF and VT notables:

- Service provider being impacted by client's and/or family member's abuse
- Client's connections to gang violence
- Unsecured weapons in the home
- Client's active alcohol and/or drug abuse
- Environmental hazards (hoarding, rodents, bug infestations)
- Service provider's exposure to blood or bodily fluids

Employees as Family Caregivers

Many of us are, or soon will be, caregivers to an elderly parent or a child with special needs. For people who are in the role of primary caregiver for a family member, this role brings a greater challenge to look after ourselves as we care for our loved one. The reason being is that we are less likely to offer the same commitment to care for ourselves. Caregivers tend to sacrifice even more of their personal time and energy when it comes to their family members.

As caregivers, we will often not have the same degree of structure or boundaries found in the employment realm. This means we won't have basic built-in reminders to take our coffee or lunch breaks, have debrief or sharing time with someone who understands, or seek longer periods of respite away from home to allow ourselves any kind of rejuvenating self-care. The sense of obligation may be greater – in that there can be higher expectations about our roles as family caregivers that our family members have of us, as well as what we have of ourselves.

We may have greater difficultly letting anyone else care for our loved one in the special ways and means that we have done. In our desire to care perfectly and lovingly, our own needs become secondary. We might well find our boundaries and ability to say "no" to increasing demands of caregiving become weaker and compassion fatigue and its exhaustive elements will gain on us.

As previously mentioned, if we are also in a work caregiving type of occupation to others and we are also caring for a loved one, we can find ourselves on a fast track to compassion fatigue by burning the candle at both ends. Wherever you reside, it's important to check out your regional health care agencies or local health units to discover health and social supports offered for families and to check if there are caregiver networks or support groups available.

Organizational Help with Compassion Fatigue and Vicarious Trauma

More organizations are providing education regarding CF and VT to staff as an important first step in orientation of new staff, especially those staff who are more vulnerable in their roles to experiencing degrees of compassion fatigue and vicarious trauma. Encouragement by management through presentations or timely in-house staff discussions to ensure staff members can recognize their own signs and symptoms of CF and VT is well worth the time.

Organizations can also create a sustainable work atmosphere that is safe for staff sharing, disclosure, and self-care. This sharing can be accomplished by encouraging in-house end-of-day staff debriefs, as well as ongoing support groups for staff where this topic is presented to encourage staff participation in ongoing wellness discussions. Specific caregiver support groups can also be formed for staff who care for a loved one at home. (See Family Care Givers below).

Francoise Mathieu, ME.D, R.P., CCC, Director of Compassion Fatigue Solutions, Inc, has studied the impact of CF and VT and how it relates to work-life balance. She states that the best way to reduce CF and VT is to work in a highly supportive work environment. This means having control over your own schedule, access to timely debriefing after a critical event, good quality supervision, and adequate training in working with difficult patients" (Mathieu, 2014).

Further, *Supporting Staff At Risk For Compassion Fatigue,* a 2012 report compiled by the Region of Peel Public Health for the cities of Brampton, Caledon and Mississauga, Ontario, addresses the nursing staff working in their Healthy Babies, Healthy Children (HBHC) program.

This report cited the need to provide support for staff to recognize and receive support for CF and VT. It was shown that staff's reflective practice, good boundary setting, and mindful self-care are indeed necessary but may be insufficient for best staff support. The report brings forward their conclusions with the following recommendations:

- Reducing compassion fatigue among staff will likely lead to better client service.
- Taking additional time to build resilience or reduce compassion fatigue could result in less direct service in the short term, but less sick-time in the longer term.
- A number of strategies to address compassion fatigue, which have been introduced in the past, may need to be modified to enhance their effectiveness.
- The orientation program for new staff, plus team and supervisory meetings, provide opportunities for introducing new interventions to all staff disciplines.

Intersection: Compassion Fatigue, Vicarious Trauma, and Organizational Change

We've established that the helping and services for employees in health care, social work, or police services are more vulnerable to experience CT, VT, and abuses. We also know that more often than ever before, we are all more involved in caring for our elderly or disabled loved ones.

The reality is becoming more obvious that any of us at varying times in our lives can become vulnerable to CF, VT, and even aspects of change fatigue given changes occurring more rapidly in our in their lives. However, systemic changes must still be carried out and while new change initiatives can hope to offer overall systemic improvements, they may also necessitate that service providers split their focus and energies on the initiatives while attempting to fully meet client needs.

The need for employees to integrate new information and processes is vital in keeping systems and services running well. However, service providers keeping up with increasing client workload demands that ultimately affect the core of a client's health and safety, can be a daunting task.

Certainly, it was a re-occurring concern that I was challenged to find solutions to as a front-line social worker, as well as in various leadership roles throughout my career. These kind of work issues can contribute to employees feeling quickly overwhelmed with their need to prioritize their own self-care to avoid CF and VT, while experiencing a growing sense of little or no control over their workloads.

Client referrals in these critical helping areas across these systems are generally on the rise and are also seen as increasing in their levels of complexity. Clients' complex mental and medical health concerns combined with clients' home safety risk factors affecting service providers in the helping arenas are:

- The exponential increase of our aging populations
- Increase in requested and/or complex service delivery referrals for the elderly as well as those living with disabilities, to allow them to stay at home or in an independent living arrangement out of residential care

- Increase in the prevalence of addiction, acquired brain injury mental health, social housing, and poverty issues
- Lack of safe homes for the transfer of abuse elderly and/or medically complex clients
- Increase in staff acting as primary caregivers for their disabled and/or elderly family

These factors can instantly and dramatically heighten levels of stress and the need for constant vigilance of staff and client safety. There are other items that we can also add to the overall impact of change and stress on managers, employees and their organizations:

- Staff turnover, attrition and additional integration of new staff requiring more specialized training/adjustment, including loss of leadership roles, puts the burden on existing employees to carry more of the work load.
- Managers, leadership and frontline service providers must attend to extra coverage and back fill with increases in staff turnover.
- Local socio-political changes affecting staff access to their work sites to allow for adequate and affordable housing with preferred proximity to community, social, educational and health care services.

These real and pressing problems will continue to challenge us. If we can focus on promoting individual and organizational practices for greater staff care in the midst of such fast and difficult changes, we can increase the entire organization's energy, sense of well-being and productivity.

Creating Workplace Community to Support Staff Needs

Most us will likely agree that a workplace atmosphere is best if it involves: gender equality, acceptance, respect, and ongoing appreciation for all positions, as well as clear communications; policies and guidelines that contribute to staff safety; ongoing education and promotion of cultural competence, creativity, control over workload and the ability to expand in one's role or advancement in leadership roles.

These are some of the key factors that provide an overall sense of workplace community. This kind of rich and rewarding community keeps managers and staff positively engaged for longer periods of time. These key factors are also instrumental in encouraging the kind of organizational openness, acceptance, and ongoing staff debriefings mentioned previously that are necessary to provide support for staff experiencing change fatigue, compassion fatigue, and vicarious traumatization.

In the workforce, we also have varying generational participants' experiences and expectations, for the Millennials (born in 1980s and later), Generation X (1962-1980), and the Baby Boomers (1945-1961). These generations are now interacting with different desires and commitments within many of the same organizations about the value and meaning of short and longer-term employment. We are seeing how these needs and expectations play out in employee recruitment, satisfaction, and retention.

There can be frustrations, judgments, and resentments resulting from various generations misperceiving one another in a negative light with views of: "He or she's too old and rigid" or, "They are young and inexperienced, seem entitled and have no value of their employment commitment" or, "He or she is just into climbing up the corporate ladder and has no sense of our team spirit" and so on. Some of these kinds of statements may have some measure of truth given the different expectations, financial needs, and other issues playing out, and some of them can be sweeping generalizations based on assumptions and misperceptions.

Though no workplace can or should be expected to meet all employee needs and expectations, in reality, many employees are trying to find their own fit in a rapidly paced and changing world with challenges to find available and accessible schooling, employment, and housing.

Sometimes there is also less commitment to stay in a job if some workplace stresses become too great too soon. A desire by many more workforce members is now becoming more focused on a healthier work/home lifestyle balance instilling a stronger sense of, "I need my allotted time off in order to be healthy and available to myself and my family. I am not a robot." Many more organizations are attempting to create support for this balance as much as possible. Given staff cutbacks in areas, this remains an ongoing challenge.

Keeping Wisdom in the Workplace

To enrich a community and keep its energy intact and moving forward is to have as many people as possible involved in meaningful activities and contributions that are respectful of skill, age, gender, or dis/ability. This can be a time when the wisdom and mentorship of experienced employees are appreciated. Experienced staff when they continue to maintain their skills in the practicalities of the work naturally can provide a communication bridge between generations of employees with their varying skills and experiences.

Mature employees acting in mentorship capacities for newer members to understand and value workplaces settings that are going through challenging transitions. Mature employees can provide the workplace with ongoing staff continuity, team stability, and wise counsel if needed within the workplace community. They can also provide a measure of guidance to assist others to examine their own strengths and find their voices in offering newer insights and solutions and to further develop their skills within their organization.

Spirituality and Ethics in the Workplace

"People are the only assets in an organization that will multiply their output to dazzling levels if their managers can demonstrate that they genuinely value not only the workers' contributions, but their very being in the work environment," (Marques, Dhiman, and King, 2007, p. 133).

Spirituality can mean something quite different to each of us. In fact, one would be hard pressed to offer a definition of spirituality that would satisfy everyone. The word spirituality can also create anxiety in some people who feel that besides politics, we shouldn't engage in conversations involving one's personal or religious beliefs.

However, over the years, there has been greater interest in incorporating aspects of our personal selves and our spiritual natures into our work rather than having a strict focus on productivity and financial outcomes. The results in many places have been an increase in staff retention with a sense of greater meaningfulness and work satisfaction. A sense of cohesiveness and connectedness in workplace communities has been heightened when employees feel their whole person is recognized (McLaughlin, 2012).

In viewing the range of meanings, spirituality's definition can be derived from institutionalized religion or theology. Though organized multi-faith expressions can be a vital part of a person's spiritual identity and practice, they do not necessarily encapsulate the breadth and wholeness of what spirituality can mean to others.

Someone can have a sense of the sacred, or be an atheist, or can view themselves as spiritual without having a clear definition of this word. Additionally, we can be all encompassing in the view that we are spiritual beings in our universal connection to nature or the oneness of all. The definitions can go on and they show, in part, the simplicity as well as the complexity of our spiritual identities – identities stemming from our families and cultures and our consciousness awareness of how we value ourselves and behave towards each other. These experiences all help to construct our understanding of what spirituality means to us.

Within the workplace, we bring in our personal fullness in the range of meanings of spirituality and it affects how we behave. In so far as common attributes of spirituality relative to our behavior in the work realm, they can be demonstrated by simple caring, compassion, and courtesy towards one another.

These offerings can also be amplified by embracing each person's strengths, unique gifts, history, and cultural diversity. This support helps create a safe and open work culture for a fuller expression of who we are. This openness and acceptance can help staff to know that when they walk through the door they are valued first for the person they are, followed by the skills they offer. The workplace then becomes one where everyone feels that they are accepted as themselves and can bring their whole being to work.

Most major religions hold key spiritual beliefs that also involve a code of conduct where core values exist like: honesty, personal responsibility, trustworthiness, justice, service, quality of work, and cooperation. Spirituality in the work setting can also be seen to value a very similar ethical code of conduct for staff.

Ethical behavior within the workplace community as a whole aspires to treat everyone fairly and ethically, regardless of title, role, or discipline. Within many work communities there are policies, principles and practices that reflect what ethical or right behavior is and what ethical decision-making involves.

An ethics framework to help guide both leadership and staff whether in business, trade, health, education, social, and private sectors is highly recommended.

When in place, it acts to deal with any ethical or stress-related issues that potentially create angst, confusion or discord for staff. To have an ethical frame of behavior to reference will:

- Preserve all staff's integrity, autonomy, and confidentiality, while also upholding communication/decision-making transparency.
- Value the collegial and/or client input for cooperative decision-making processes
- Ensure the right use of employer's authoritative power
- Address the need for clear, common and realistic goals for the work community.

Humor and Playfulness at Work

Work has to have some measure of fun to create a healthy balance. Even in workplaces where there is a lot of energy going out to manage very difficult health or social challenges in people's lives, humor is a needed form of release. Humor and play are integral to lifting our spirits and revitalizing our health and wellness, no matter if we are at work or at home.

Lightness of heart, mind, and spirit through humor and play can offer us the balance we need to let go and let up on any excess pressure, fear, grief, upset, or work and family responsibilities that can consume us. Humor and play also bring out our inner child's creativity and spontaneity – and are part of how we can enrich our imaginations.

When we cannot actively tap into our own imaginations easily, we can become irritated, frustrated, or even depressed. The ability to visualize, imagine, and play is a basic human expression that needs a natural outlet.

As adults and parents, we know the absolute value of encouraging a child's imagination to increase cognitive development, learning, and healthy socialization. Children who sit in front of a TV all day are not being stimulated to use their own imaginations and creative energies. The restlessness and irritation that can come from that constant screen viewing contributes to increased outward expression of a frustration and anger.

Similarly, adults who are subjected to excessive rote routines, or who have too much responsibility and stresses – if not infused with creative or playful energy – will eventually feel blocked, frustrated, and angry. Activities that can include anything from solution focused problem-solving, positive participation in development of new systems that are truly of interest, or expressing any of the arts, will allow feelings of creativity and lightness to emerge again and it will help bring out our natural joy of living.

Helpful Websites

There are many helpful websites that offer free downloads for information and self-testing, education, and support. These are a few:

- **Traumatology Institute, Canada:**
  - http//psychink.com/ Traumatology Institute - In-Class training for Trauma and Compassion
- **Stamm's (2005) Professional Quality of Life Scale** (ProQOL) (developed from Figley (1996):
  - http//www.compassionfatigue.org/pages/ProQOL ManualOct05.pdf
- **Compassion Fatigue Among Registered Nurses**. Community Health (Maralon Bevens, RN.MN, University of Lethbridge, 2010):
  - http//www.chnc.ca/documents/compassionfatigue amongregisterednurses-presentations.pdf

- **Compassion Fatigue Awareness Project,** (2008): www.compassionfatigue.org
- **Compassion Fatigue and Compassion Satisfaction among Police Officers: An Understudied Topic**
  - o www.omicsonline.com/.../compassion-fatigue-and-compassion-satisfaction
- **Managing Transitions. Making the Most of Change.** William Bridges, Ph.D., Da Capo Press. (1991-2009)
- **Family Caregivers BC**
  - o www.familycaregiversbc.ca
- **Home and Community Care, Vancouver Coastal Health**
  - o www.vch.ca
- **Compassion Fatigue and Family Caregivers**
  - o www.familycaregiversbc.ca/wp-content/.../03/Compassion-Fatigue.pdf
- **British Columbia Association of Social Workers (BCASW)**

Self-Care: An Ethical Imperative (2011)
  - o www.bcasw.org/wp-content/uploads/.../Perspectives-January-2011.pdf
- **Vince Gowmon, Training For A New World.** www.vincegowmon.com
- **101 Ways to Use Humor at Work.** www.humorthatworks.com

- **Auntie Acid.** www.auntyacid.com

In the next chapter, we will examine how we can further help ourselves when we are at work or at home by exploring and strengthening our personal and collective resilience.

Chapter 7
Building Our Resilience

Resilience

Resilience is part of our own inner self-care and self-sustaining mechanism. It's how we bounce back from difficult experiences. It is the process of adapting well in the face of adversity, trauma, tragedy, threats, or even significant sources of stress — such as family and relationship problems, serious health problems, or workplace and financial stressors. It shows us the strength of our spirit in the face of powerful odds.

Research has shown that resilience is more of a routine response for most of us. It involves behaviors, thoughts, and actions that can be learned and developed in anyone (American Psychological Association, 2016). That's good news because we can then strengthen what already exists.

We know that our resilience begins when our body is forming our earliest bio-neuro coding for our cognitive functions. This coding is at a time when we begin evolving interactions with our outer environment and our understanding of what's initially needed for our survival.

Resilience then grows to encompass a dual understanding of what we feel we need to achieve for a sense of happiness within us, as well as how we are able to use the resources around us. We need to survive, and we also want to thrive.

Outer Resilience Resources
Our Primary Relationships

One of the primary resource factors contributing to resilience is our ability to form nourishing, loving relationships.

Relationship building begins with our family relationships, especially with our parents and siblings. These relationships impart a powerful and lifelong imprint for each of us. They are critical in our experience of being nourished and supported and are where trust building, belonging, and behavior modelling occurs. Maintaining positive relationships with supportive family, friends, and colleagues is perhaps the most important resilience element of all.

Our Spiritual, Cultural, or Community Support

When change comes into our lives, we cope best with a sense of community. Connecting with supportive people that share a circle of support with a common activity, cultural, or spiritual bond becomes vital in our resilience to withstand changes. This sharing and mirroring helps keep things in perspective and gently reminds us of our essential belongingness, sacredness, and worthiness in the world. This important support can also strengthen some of our inner resilience reserves below.

Inner Resilience Resources

Acknowledge Our Strengths

The ability to have insight into our own strengths is essential. It helps us keep a positive perspective and confidence in ourselves no matter the circumstances. We saw earlier that there is a human tendency to default to the negative, and we can counteract this negative default by consciously affirming our strengths and skills.

Accomplishing Realistic Goals

It can be easier to set short-term, even daily, and longer-term goals that can be successfully reached in realistic time frames. Since so much is now changing in our world, longer-term goals may need to be adjusted more often. If we start with the smaller, easier goals that we know we can accomplish, we can build upon each achievement with a "congratulations" to ourselves!

Solution-Focused Problem Solving

Solution-focused problem solving is the ability to appreciate what is actively working in our lives and what our strengths are instead of focusing on our deficits. In this way, we look at what we want rather than what we don't want for our resolutions. This way of problem solving examines any exceptions as to when the problem is not occurring and seeing if we can use those exceptions to work towards our solutions in a different way. (Priest and Gass, 1997).

Emotional Self-Management

Emotional self-management is our ability to recognize the full range of our feelings and emotions, and be motivated to manage them effectively. This learning can include strengthening ourselves emotionally, particularly in those situations that trigger our anger and any tendency to blame. Emotional self-management gives us more emotional intelligence in trusting ourselves to manage any situation. The overall result is a boost in our self-esteem and confidence.

Broader Resilience Resources

Cultural Competency

An important strategy for building resiliency is cultivating cultural competency to foster our greater community. Cultural competency involves learning about the specific behaviors, attitudes, and spiritual or religious practices of those with whom we live and work. By being genuinely interested in knowing about others, we show respect for their culture and enhance interactions in our diverse communities. When we embrace openness and seek to become culturally competent, we build more strength and significantly increase the sense of global unity.

In viewing how people practice self-care in times of significant change, it's essential to appreciate that individuals and entire communities do not all react or respond the same way to traumatic events or stresses. There can be striking differences in people's perceptions, their desire or ability to reach out for help, or to openly discuss their experiences. Developing cultural competency needs to be ongoing as people are leaving their homes in different kinds of situations, and sometimes leaving with little or no preparation to enter a new cultural experience.

LGBTQ2S Community

Cultural competency also involves understanding and honoring LGBTQ2S (Lesbian, Gay, Bisexual, Transgendered, Queer and Two-Spirited) community members. Across the globe, individuals are still being denied recognition, inclusion, and respect. Many of our LGBTQ2S peoples have been exiled from their own religious, spiritual, or community cultures of origin. Many have chosen to leave for their own mental, spiritual, and physical wellness and safety.

Inclusive acceptance of sexual orientation and gender identity is still being battled in real life-and-death situations in some countries where homophobia remains pervasively alive in its many forms. There still is a profound lack of knowledge in the world about the breadth and beauty of the expression of human sexuality, which is also connected to the vitality of the human spirit.

Social Determinants of Health

In terms of the wide array of elements encompassing holistic self-care in this book, the Public Health Agency of Canada (PHAC), as part of the Canadian government's Health Portfolio, has named key health key determinants linked to resiliency factors worth addressing when assessing people's quality of life. They are important in and of themselves and are also interrelated to one's overall health and wellness. The following determinants are extrapolated from the PHAC's website. For additional reading, visit:

http://www.phac-aspc.gc.ca/ph-sp/determinants/index-eng.php#key_determinants.

Income and Social Status

Higher income and social status generally equate to higher health status. Research has demonstrated to a large extent that people with higher incomes and social status experience more control over their lives, particularly in stressful times, and feel better equipped to act on their own behalf.

Social Support Networks

Better health is shown in communities that support families through friends, social networks, and healthy family ties. Facing adversity and solving problems is easier with strong social support networks, and aids in people feeling they have a greater measure of control over their own lives.

Education and Literacy

People who are able to acquire a higher education and literacy level not only stay gainfully employed longer with more chance of job satisfaction, but they also have knowledge and skills that allow them to understand information to support their health, to better problem solve, and master life's circumstances.

Employment/Working Conditions

High-risk jobs are usually more stressful and result in higher numbers of accidents and injuries. Improved working conditions result in fewer accidents, greater employee work satisfaction, staff retention, and a healthier team.

Social Environments

The strength and health of any community, from local to regional, stems from the varied ways and means that people give, share, and form bonds with one another. It is mirrored in the organizations and institutions that are created and sustained for the community's cohesiveness. This cohesiveness acknowledges the degree of diversity, and the work that's being done towards healthier, safer, and more supportive working relationships.

Physical Environments

Communities we live in affect us physically and psychologically. If these communities are carefully designed via transportation routes and other factors to avoid or effectively deal with exposure to contaminants in water, air, and soil, it can protect people from adverse health ailments such as gastrointestinal illnesses, birth defects, and cancer.

Personal Health Practices and Coping Skills

Personal life choices are affected by socio-environmental influences at home, work, school, and play. Those influences affect the health-related decisions that people make to enhance their own health and practice disease prevention. The better the interventions, the better the overall choices people will make for good health.

Healthy Child Development

Our life cycle experiences, from conception to age six, are the most critical for healthy development of brain neurology. Ensuring positive stimulation at this stage and onward will ensure greater success for learning and behavior into adulthood.

Biology and Genetic Endowment

Health status can also be affected by one's genetic predisposition to specific diseases or health issues, an important factor for our increased awareness.

Health Services

Population health services look at the whole population's needs to achieve health and promote disease prevention. It is part of the overall health services continuum that also involves treatment and secondary prevention.

Gender

Although concepts and norms of gender are being challenged in worldwide culture, according to the PHAC's website, gender is referenced as, "the array of society-determined roles, personality traits, attitudes, behaviors, values, relative power and influence that society ascribes to the two sexes on a differential basis." What this determinant attempts to underscore is that there are health issues which are still considered to be a result or function of gendered norms. These norms are still influencing the greater continuum of health care practices and policies.

Culture

The dominant cultural values that can negatively contribute to marginalization, cultural and language debasement, or stigmatization can create health risks for other cultures, and discourage access to culturally appropriate health care services.

Social Determinants of Indigenous Peoples' Health

The impact on First Nations, Inuit, and Metis peoples from colonization, separation of families through residential schools, forced settlements and reserves, and the impact of overall cultural losses, has been deleterious to say the least. The Indigenous peoples' resilience cannot be understated – it is a testimony to their strength of culture, spirit, and soul, particularly when the generational traumas from these experiences are still having an impact.

Extensive research done by the National Collaborating Centre for Aboriginal Health (NCCAH) has shown that social determinants of health of Indigenous peoples differ to varying and sometimes substantive degrees from the non-Aboriginal determinants, which tend to be more siloed in treatment, prevention, and delivery approaches.

The Indigenous concept of health is predominantly viewed in an interrelated holistic approach that reflects the mental, emotional, physical, and spiritual realms of health over a lifelong trajectory. In specific regard to physical environments, an area that is primary in healthy outcomes for populations, housing shortages and the poor quality of existing homes has created overcrowding on the forced reserves and settlements, as well as homelessness for Aboriginals in urban areas.

- *Health Inequalities and Social Determinants of Aboriginal Peoples' Health. (www.nccah-ccnsa.ca)*

http://www.nccah-ccnsa.ca/28/Social_Determinants.nccah

- Reading, C, Ph.D., and Wien, F., Ph.D. (2009, 2013) *Health Inequalities And Social Determinants Of Aboriginal Peoples' Health,* in National Collaborating Centre For Aboriginal Health, University of Northern British Columbia, Prince George, BC (page 12) http://www.nccah-ccnsa.ca/Publications/Lists/Publications/Attachments/46/health_inequalities_EN_web.pdf

Health Canada's *A Statistical Profile on the Health of First Nations in Canada: Determinants of Health, 2006-2010*, provides census data showing that:

"*Over one-quarter (28%) of Registered Indian households in First Nations communities fell below the adequacy standard—they were considered by their residents as requiring major repairs. This was more than 10 times the percentage for non-Aboriginal households outside of First Nations communities… In addition, 12% of Registered Indian households fell below the suitability standard—their homes did not have enough bedrooms for the size and make up of those living in the home.*" *(p. 48)*

There are still obvious distinct and severe disparities for Indigenous peoples in maintaining healthy lives. There is a disproportionate lack of employment opportunities, education, access to healthy food, water, and higher levels of poverty. Much collaborative work on a national level is urgently necessary in some areas and will be long term in rectifying the current state of imbalance of the health standards of Indigenous peoples.

Nutrition in Self-Care

Good nutrition is a cornerstone of optimal health. Many of us have our own cultural preferences in our relationship with food as it can hold spiritual symbolism and meaning for our health and wellness.

In some spiritual life practices, like Ayurveda, our body is a sacred temple. What we place in it needs to not only nourish our body it must also honor and support our inner higher spiritual being that is ultimately connected to the Divine, and it is an important acknowledgement of our need to be mindful in our eating.

This mindfulness is necessary because, as food is alive with its own life force, it makes sense to choose more natural foods over packaged and processed foods that has far less energy to nourish our bodies.

In British Columbia and in other parts of the world, First Nations or Aboriginal peoples are culturally connected to the land, water, fish, wildlife, and plant life. Food holds traditional spiritual meaning and recognition of the need to preserve and protect the environment and its inhabitants. Traditional harvesting of animals, fish, and plants for maximum nutritional benefits is carried out with mindfulness of the need for self-sufficiency with the preservation and conservation of life.

"Go to the land and waters to find your first foods. Be active in exercising your right to hunt, fish, harvest, and gather in your territory. Ask the old people and the traditional and environmental knowledge keepers how to do this in a good way. It will be good for the mind, body, and spirit and contribute to a self-reliant future" (First Nations Health Authority, 2016). RD Program Nutritionist, FNHA

What Should I Eat?

For many of us, our relationship with food can be complex and even confusing at times. There seems to be so much information and misinformation as to what we should and should not be eating for our best health. We have developing issues regarding whether to eat gluten-free or not, the nature of allergies to food, concerns regarding genetically modified organism (GMO) foods, the range of questionable food additives, and the impact on our digestive systems. The overall degradation of the quality of our food, and a tremendous influx of health food supplements we are encouraged to use and even overuse to make up that difference have added to our confusion.

Dr. Vandana Shiva, author, activist and scientific advisor, has researched and lectured globally on the nature and direction of the world's changes occurring in our food and nutritional resources, as well as the concerns involving GMO foods. Shiva (2014) cites the urgent need to return to the rich diversity we once had of the 8,500 species of foods that our body really needs for optimal nutritional health.

There is an increase in the belief that there is more nutritious bang for your buck when eating whole, organic, and grass-fed foods. However, there is an unfortunate increase in cost for many of these foods, making these nourishing foods cost prohibitive for many people. People living on low incomes often must choose lower cost, high sugar, fatty, and carbohydrate-rich foods to survive. We know in healing and health care services good whole nutrition is strongly encouraged for disease prevention. Diabetes Type 2 Disease, as only one example, has been linked to poverty.

We know the level of energy related to the quality of food's nutrition affects every cell of our brain and body to preserve our mental recall, learning, physical responses, and emotional stasis. Emotionally, food also becomes a means of coping when stress levels rise. We often go for quick comfort and too often sugar is one of the most available substances to momentarily quell the stress response.

Andrew Weil, author of *Spontaneous Healing* (1995) agrees that our diet is a significant part of maintaining our longevity and adds that,

"Fortunately or unfortunately, we live in a world that tempts us with a great variety and abundance of food, and many of us eat not to satisfy hunger but to ally anxiety, depression, and boredom, to provide a substitute for emotional nourishment, or to try to fill an inner void" (p. 170).

In one of my previous social work positions working with people with a variety of addictions, the pervasive negative impact of sugar became quickly apparent. Like the opioids morphine and heroin, sugar has a similar effect on certain pathways of the brain, which results in a sense of craving for more of the substance when its ingestion is followed by cessation.

Over time, our ability to regulate that substance becomes diminished and we need more of it to get the same dopamine pleasure effect to calm us. Our ability to resist the temptation of sugary substances in junk food ends up not being about a lack of willpower, but about the development of our brain's and body's response – a response that resembles that of a drug addiction. It's no small wonder many of us have found ourselves on the continuum of disordered eating.

Moving towards healthier eating habits takes time. It takes gentle patience to learn about the role of food in our lives and how we can become aware of what we are eating – what it is and is not giving us – and why we are drawn to certain foods and substances. In *Super Brain* (2012), Deepak Chopra and Rudolph E. Tanzi examine the issue of disordered eating on the spectrum from anorexia to obesity. They urge that in order to help ourselves come back into a balanced state, we need to know that rebalancing the brain is the key to the solution.

"The key is to bring our brain into balance, then use its ability to balance everything – hormones, hunger, cravings, and habits. Your weight is all in your head because, ultimately, your body is in your head. That is, the brain lies at the source of all bodily functions, and your mind lies at the source of your brain" (p. 97).

They highlight that if an eating imbalance is occurring, accommodating that imbalance by continuing to adapt or work around our underweight or overweight creates even a greater imbalance. They make this argument because "imbalance feeds more imbalance" and it becomes a true vicious circle – ultimately resulting in grave health consequences. Chopra and Tanzi urge readers to:

- Stop fighting with yourself
- Give up diet foods
- Work to restore balance in areas that create imbalance – stress, emotions, and sleep

Again, this is where we need to consciously try to make time to ask and find out what is going on within ourselves. What are our stress trigger points, or any areas of unresolved emotional issues? This is a time when we need to become gentle and compassionate observers. When we recognize a change is needed though, it is also time to take action on our own behalf.

Detoxification

Depending on the goals people participate in detoxification processes for a variety of reasons. Detoxification or withdrawing from certain food groups sometimes with the increase in other food categories and methods of preparation (eg. juicing) and sometimes with the addition of specific herbs to promote toxins to be released.

Detoxifying the body can reveal much information concerning potential allergies and other manifestations of physical irritants and ailments. The overall benefits can include: weight loss, clearer thinking, increased energy, stronger immunity, clearer skin and shinier hair, improved sleep patterns, decreased muscle or joint pain and the list goes on.

There are many forms of detoxifications that can last for several days or weeks depending on your specific goals, degree of health to manage a specific detox plan and any life-style challenges. It can be easily confusing to figure out what kind of detoxification is best for each of us and therefore it is important to research any plan and consult fully with your physician and/or the product or processes involved.

Additional information and support for any of us in our nutritional needs can also come from a local community health center's dietitian, a community holistic nutritionist, a naturopath, and possibly a support group if we feel we are somewhere on the continuum of disordered eating. We may need to get specific organ, gland, blood, or hormonal tests (sometimes through saliva) to find out more detailed specifics about how we are functioning and what we need if we are out of balance or in nutritional deficiency.

Herbs and Spices

I've included herbs and spices as a seemingly smaller food group, but it is actually an area of enormous information and assistance to our health care. Herbs and spices offer significant rewards for mind and body functional enhancement, immune boosting, healing, detoxification and are a contributing factor in overall healthy living and aging.

Globally, the ancients and Aboriginal peoples were the first herbalists in their use of thousands of plants, shrubs, and trees with specific rituals to purify and heal the body, mind, and spirit. We routinely benefit ourselves today by the use of Echinacea, goldenseal, ginseng, gotu kola, garlic, ginger, lavender, pepper, cloves, nutmeg, turmeric, chilies, to name but a fraction of helpful herbs and spices (Mindell, 1992).

Within our communities there are skilled herbalists and many naturopaths that have studied the work passed over centuries who can provide us with this beneficial information to improve health and wellness. There are also community and online courses for learning the role of specific food groups, their impact, and how we can keep ourselves optimally functioning.

David "Avocado" Wolfe's online *Living Nutrition* e-course through the BodyMind Institute is very information, interesting, and easy to follow. (https://bodymindinstitute.com/the-exclusive-**david-wolfe**-nutrition-certifi...)

Information on First Nations Medicine can also be found at:

- Turtle Island Native Network: Healing and Wellness http://www.turtleisland.org/healing/healing-wellness.htm
- Moerman, Daniel. *Native American Ethnobotany* (Timber Press, 1998) and online http://www.herbmed.org/links.html
- Cichoke, Anthony J. (2001) *Secrets of Native American Herbal Remedies A Comprehensive Guide to the Native American Tradition of Using Herbs and the Mind/body/spirit Connection for Improving Health and Well-being.* Penguin Publishers.

The Vibrational Color of Food

There's a reason your parents said, "Eat your greens!" Food also has an energetic vibration and its color is certainly an aspect of how food affects our body's energy systems. For example:

Green foods: broccoli, asparagus, olives, avocado, pears, limes, and green grapes offer support and blood purification.

Red foods: red apples, tomatoes, strawberries, offer antioxidants and beta-carotene to neutralize free radicals.

Orange foods: carrots, squash, sweet potatoes, oranges, apricots, melons, egg yolk, turmeric, and ginger also provide minerals, antioxidants and Vitamin C.

Yellow foods: yellow peppers, parsnips, yams, grapefruit, lemons, pineapples, and pears offer more sun-derived antioxidants, plus iron, magnesium, zinc, Vitamins B, and E.

Blue foods: seaweed, asparagus, plums, blueberries, and boysenberries are rich in vital minerals and antioxidants.

Purple foods: eggplant, plums, purple grapes, blackberries, and lavender help to calm mental and nervous system disorders.

Some foods have several colors associated with them because they change color when cooked.

Aside from the various authors and other resources we can access, we need to structure a healthy food plan that works for each of us, given our lifestyles, our preferences, our coping methods, our income, and the kind of supports around us.

Blessing Our Food

Blessing food, as in saying grace, may seem unnecessary or far too traditional or old fashioned, unless you are in keeping with a faith that maintains the practice of saying a blessing or prayer before eating. Actually, blessing food increases the vibration of the food we eat. When we send positive regard or simple appreciation for our food, it absorbs the positive energy we send to it and that also helps nourish our bodies better.

As often as one can remember, it is good to give gratitude to food and/or to the animal if you eat meat to honor its life, and ask that the food provide you with maximum nourishment. It's a simple thing to do and it allows a sense of sacredness to become part of our eating habits.

An example of a simple blessing is, "We offer gratitude for this food, water, etc., (and to this animal for its life) and may this food provide us with all the nourishment we need."

One of the most important factors, along with caring that the food we eat provides us with good nutrition for our wellness, is also the quantity and quality of the water available to us.

Water

As we are primarily composed of water, it's important to ensure we are adequately hydrated with filtered, non-fluoridated, primarily alkaline water throughout the day. Sometimes, instead of feeling hungry we are really feeling thirsty.

Brenda Watson, author of *The Detox Strategy* (2008), suggests that we drink half our body weight in ounces of water per day. For example, a 140-pound person would drink 70 ounces. Drinking more water per day gives us a number of positive health benefits:

- Increases metabolism and energy
- Acts as natural daily detoxification
- When adding lemon juice or apple cider vinegar to water, it helps alkalize the body, increases bile, and flushes out the kidneys
- Helps prevent constipation
- Improves skin tone

Water Quality

Where I live, our watershed has no added fluoridated water (http://yourwatermatters.com/vancouver-water/top-11-questions-about-metro-vancouver-tap-water/.) There continues to be ongoing concerned debate on the efficacy of fluoridation in water to protect and strengthen tooth enamel against acid erosion, plaque, and bacteria. Many Canadian dental associations offer support for measured use of fluoride.

The Canadian Dental Association Inc. (cdc.adc.ca) also supports the use of fluoride being added to water, "*to protect all members of the community from tooth decay. Community water fluoridation is a safe and effective way of preventing tooth decay at a low cost."*

However, other studies show that fluoride has a significant calcification effect on the pineal gland because fluoride accumulates easily in the brain. This accumulation causes the pineal gland to become less functional with notable decreased levels of melatonin, a serotonin-derived hormone that regulates our bio-rhythms like our sleep-wake cycles (Luke, 2001).

As mentioned in chapter 1, the pineal gland is one of the seven powerful chakras in our body and is sometimes called the seat of the soul. It is associated with our brain's functions. Researchers for some years have expressed concern regarding the connection of sodium fluoride's impact on the pineal gland with the development of cognitive diminishment, decreased insight and even Alzheimer's disease. Independent of this section, readers are encouraged to research this issue further to determine their own conclusions. Pros and cons are discussed in part in the following discussions:

- "Should Canadian Communities continue to fluoridate water?" *(healthydebate.ca/2015/07/topic/evidence-for-fluoridated-water),*
- The Fluoride Debate-CBC Archives *(www.cbc.ca/archives/topic/the-**fluoride**-debate)*
- Pineal Gland, from Wikipedia *https://en.wikipedia.org/wiki/Pineal_gland*
- "Pineal gland calcification and the defective sense of direction." C.R. Bayliss, N.L Bishop and R.C. Fowler. British Medical Journal. Volume 291, p 21-28 December 1985. (https://www.ncbi.nlm.nih.gov/pmc/articles/PMC1419 179/pdf/bmjcred00479-0018.pdf)

If one is concerned enough to want to explore recovery from any degree of decalcification of the pineal gland and add more health into one's diet, consult an accredited herbalist, nutritionist or health food consultant.

Additionally, there are available foods to assist in whole body wellness that assist in pineal gland decalcification such as, walnuts, neem extract, spirulina, apple cider vinegar, coconut oil, turmeric, and ginger as a few examples.

By focusing on areas of nutrition, hydration, coping, and stress reduction, we can do well along our nutritional path, but become undermined by another critical part of our self-care – getting adequate sleep.

The Importance of Sleep

"How are you this morning?" Not bad, just a little sleep deprived …"

Adequate sleep is critical for the body's continued need for tissue repair and for all-around restorative health. Each of us has an internal circadian rhythm 24-hour body clock that is affected by sunlight, temperature, our behavior, and lifestyle. This master clock also controls the production of the hormone melatonin, significant for a good night's sleep (National Institute of General Medical Sciences, 2016).

The literature on sleep shows we can differ individually in terms of adequate number of hours of sleep we need to function well according to: our age, lifestyle, work routines, physical activity, stress, depression, anxiety issues, or the particular life stage we are in that may result in hormonal fluctuations.

According to *The Canadian Sleep Review Current Issues, Attitudes and Advice to Canadians* (2016), *"Many Canadians are functioning with chronic sleep debt, a pervasive issue and a significant health concern for many people, affecting many segments of the population"*.

The Mayo Clinic reports that a consistent lack of sleep – less than five hours for men and less than six hours for women – is also a factor in weight gain. A natural response to lack of sleep is to participate in less activity. A lack of sleep response is also to increase food and other sugar substances to boost energy levels. This response is because sleep affects hormones associated with regulating the appetite – ghrelin and leptin (Hensrud, 2015).

The Canadian Sleep Review (2016) also cites that Canadians do not give sleep their highest priority, yet we are quite knowledgeable about the dos and don'ts when planning on getting a good sleep. Specific sleep disruptions are related to: relationship discord issues, willingness to sacrifice sleep to fit in other activities, work and or home life stresses, inability to adapt to ongoing home and work changes, long distances commuting between work and home, excessive exposure to computer screens, working more than one job, illnesses, change of diet, and hormonal changes. All these areas adversely affect sleep and in turn the lack of sleep contributes to significant performance, and health and safety issues.

"An alarming 20 percent of Canadians admit to falling asleep at the wheel at least once over the last year. Studies also suggest fatigue is a factor in about 15 percent of motor vehicle collisions, resulting in about 400 deaths and 2,100 serious injuries every year. (Canada Safety Council, 2009).

Insomnia

Insomnia is specific and covers patterns that can occur even when one makes an effort to sleep well. The Canadian Sleep Society addresses insomnia sleep issues that primarily stem from anxiety, depression, and stress, but can also include chronic pain and side effects from the use of over-the-counter medication.

The issues are: difficulty falling asleep, waking up in the middle of the night and not being able to fall back asleep, poor quality of sleep if sleeping too lightly, and waking up too early in the morning and not getting back to sleep. Chronic sleep deprivation can be a singular contributing source of depression (Morin, 2014).

Insomnia can occur when we are in transition of any kind, as our inner energies will shift and change. This occurs when someone or an animal close to us dies, we move to a new home, or change jobs.

Sudden sleep changes can also occur with transitions connected to emotional and spiritual insights. These insights can happen when we go through intense therapy to resolve traumas and/or step away from addictions. It can also happen when we are touched by an event or a situation that triggers these deeper insights and shifts and opens up our energy system – meaning any one of our chakras will become unblocked and more energy begins to run through us.

These openings can be subtle or dramatic, but opening to new insights, feelings, or long-forgotten memories can be as aspect of our spiritual growth. More energy can start moving through our mind and body as we open up to our spiritual senses. These experiences, although positive, can also be painful when we let go. They can be disruptive and throw us off our normal routine.

The disruptions do calm down after a while when our mind, emotions, and physical bodies begin to catch up to the spiritual growth that's occurring. We can rebalance, but we still need to try and make personal and environmental adjustments to cope. We also need to ask for the right help.

Recommendations for Improved Sleep

First, we need to prioritize sleep. We need to see it as paramount in our daily plan for good self-care and make changes to get the required sleep we need. Sleep deprivation over time becomes too costly to our functioning. There are various avenues to improve sleep including: prescription medication (short-term only as drug dependency is real and dangerous), behavior therapy, and herbal supplements, which are not regulated. Before spending money on prescriptions or other supplements:

1. Ensure your bedroom is as dark, quiet, and comfortable as possible.
2. Avoid all stimulants like caffeine or nicotine a few hours before bedtime.
3. Avoid drinking alcohol several hours before bedtime, as you will likely wake up too early.
4. Avoid TV news as it tends to increase anxiety and stress and we're more vulnerable to its impact at bedtime.
5. Exercise later on in the day to relax and tire you.
6. Journal your concerns of the day to avoid ruminating on them.

7. Read before going to bed to divert attention from the day, but avoid computer screens and tablets.
8. Eat a low-carb snack before bedtime to avoid a drop in blood sugar and wakefulness during the night.
9. Meditate or deep breathe at bedtime. Focusing solely on the breath is highly effective in bringing calm. Some people find it highly effective to count down from 20 when focusing your mind on your breath at bedtime.
10. Get up at the same time every morning, if possible.
11. Take some herbal tea that is meant to calm. Consult with an herbalist or holistic health consultant.
12. Take a vacation.
13. Use prayer.
14. Meditate.
15. Sleep App: "mysleepbutton.com", is an application recently developed by a Simon Fraser University Professor, Dr. Luc Beaudoin, and has already shown considerable promise for those suffering from sleep difficulties. This app also garnered the interest of Oprah Winfrey and it was showcased on Global News, May 3rd, 2017 (http://globalnews.ca/news/3423143/b-c-professors-sleep-technique-gets-attention-from-oprah/)

Changes to develop or retain more hours of sleep can take time and test your patience. It's good to consult with your physician, a counsellor, psychologist, or a trusted friend to share and get more information to reduce anxiety, stress, grief, or depression. It's too uncomfortable and emotionally painful to suffer through nights of sleep upheaval and deprivation and not seek help.

Physical Exercise

The topic of exercise is a large area of information but certainly a vital one to keep our bodies working optimally. How much, how often, when and what form of exercise that is considered necessary and sustainable for one's self-care varies as to each individual's state of health, physical build and capability, interest, life-style, specific goals, and any other factors.

I have spent my life participating in all kinds of activities for enjoyment and to use my energy to ensure a balanced lifestyle and manage the stresses that have occurred. Health and exercise regimes change over time. At this time in my life, I try to minimally ensure a daily walking and/or cycling routine with strength maintenance exercises three days a week at the gym.

Given the vastness of the subject, I won't be delving into this topic within this writing but would offer to suggest that each of us start what is simple and reasonable and what we already know of ourselves. Start any new routine with what is easiest and build from there. Buddy up with someone who has similar goals to encourage us to keep up our healthy routines. If necessary, we should further consult with those who can assist us to make the best choices for strength and health with any current physical, emotional or mental challenges we are working with.

Getting through difficult times that create upheavals can also involve going deeper within ourselves to bring forward more of our inner wisdom. If we can possibly make more time to spend with ourselves, it can help in numerous ways. The next chapter will look more closely at strengthening our inner reserves.

Chapter 8
Increasing Strength Through Inner Doors

Compassion is Strength

There are times where we just want to be alone and quiet with ourselves in deeper reflection to get to know ourselves better, or to just take a timeout from daily stresses. Taking time away might seem almost impossible if we are feeling completely stretched for time with a lot of responsibilities related to our job, family, or community involvement.

If we are actually able to take time for contemplation, and re-energizing, beginning with short time frames of a few minutes to a few hours here and there, we can gradually extend it to longer time frames to make it really worthwhile. More relaxed quiet time brings an increase in our awareness, objectivity, and problem solving while it refreshes our senses. Taking time for ourselves allows us to see if we are really taking our lives forward in the direction we want or if we need to make some changes.

I have a friend who, in past years, would spend months on top of a forest fire lookout in the Yukon Territory. These were incredibly solitary times for her, but she told me they were also times of personal deepening and connecting to nature and what her own spirituality held for her. Communing at length with our natural surroundings is to me one of the best forms of solace and retreat.

Perhaps some of us have spent significant times in various kinds of retreats, in or out of our country of origin, and found we've returned with a significantly changed view of life, of our relationships, and ourselves. I certainly have practiced taking vacation weeks as forms of needed change and retreat into restful solitude and learning, and also greatly enjoy stepping out of retreat mode to meet new people in different environments.

There are many ways to go about finding our own inner revelations in places of rest and rejuvenation. The following information and suggestions are offered, as they have been helpful to others and to me. Since we hold many answers to life's hurdles inside ourselves, if we dedicate enough time and space, we can practice accessing those insights much more easily and strengthen our confidence and self-reliance in the process. These are some vital areas to consider when we want to see our lives unfold more peacefully. It starts inside of us.

Every Feeling Counts

"To ignore, repress, or dismiss our feelings is to fail to listen to the stirrings of the Spirit within our emotional life."
– Brennan Manning

One of the most difficult things we do in our lifetime is learning to accept all of our feelings, even the gnarliest ones. In Canadian culture, we tend towards a stoic style of showing, or not showing our feelings, especially with feelings of grief, hurt, sadness, fear, guilt, or embarrassment. If we do express some of these feelings, there can be a lingering concern of whether we are expressing our feelings appropriately or if we are at risk being considered too sensitive, or too emotional, too this or too that.

Generally, most people tend to avoid the overall experience of feeling awkward and vulnerable when experiencing or expressing their feelings. Vulnerability has had many public commentaries in recent years to bring to light that there is strength in showing our lovingness, tenderness, anxiety, shyness, awkwardness, uncertainty, confusion, and other feelings that might make us fear being unprotected and at risk of being hurt or diminished in some way. To live our lives to the fullest in the breadth and richness of our own humanity means taking risks in moving beyond our emotional fears and risk appearing weak, soft, foolish, uninformed, unintelligent, or simply not part of the group.

Our feelings are integrally connected to all of our energy systems, as shown in previous chapters, and they have decisive impact on all parts of our human functioning. If we choose to open as fully as we can to deeper experiences involving all of our feelings and our heart's deeper expressions, we will feel uncertain and vulnerable. It is in those moments, if we decide to remain for a time, when we also add more strength and courage into our lives.

Listening to Your Heart's Wisdom

"Know that when the mind is not connected to the heart, ego rules."

– Kuthumi

I can say without hesitation that the heart's energy has the power to dramatically transform and soften the mind to open to thoughts of kindness, understanding and compassion. If we leave our heart out and we just listen to the mind to solve all issues, the mind tends to like to distract itself through the ego. The ego easily shifts to fear, confusion, and even disaster thinking when it's not sure about something or when it is not linked up to the heart's intuitive wisdom.

Listening to my heart has been a primary part of my inner GPS. Since early childhood, I have felt a sense of knowing from my heart and I have tried to listen as much as possible to its intuitive voice to guide me through life's challenges.

Present day science is now catching up with our inner spiritual knowingness as it now recognizes that the heart actually contains a "little brain" (Braden, 2015, p.11-14). Specifically, the heart brain sends information electrically to our cranial brain via its own specialized neurites, which are also found in the cranial brain, in order for the heart brain to perform its many functions.

Notably, it promotes states of deeper intuition and contributes to our precognitive abilities. The heart brain can work independently from the cranial brain to provide cognition and awareness of our individual inner worlds and outer experiences. Additionally, and at minimum, the heart brain serves to provide its own independent recall and memory.

This is where the age-old phrase "wisdom of the heart" is most real and wonderful. It's what many of us have always known when looking into our hearts for guidance. In terms of intelligent collaboration, the heart also acts in harmony with the brain for tasks that benefit both organs in providing the specific service needed in each moment.

On a feeling level, how do we open our hearts more? Sometimes we might feel we are already open enough when in fact, we are still acting in protective ways as habit from past rejections or pain from grief and traumatic losses. We may not be aware we have emotionally armored ourselves in an attempt preserve some sense of safety and control. This kind of self-preservation can keep our hearts feeling unfulfilled because we are unconsciously or otherwise keeping people and love at a distance.

In other moments, we have opened our hearts when significant losses or deaths have occurred. These events have become triggering, painful, and transforming times where we have felt cracked open to depths within ourselves – eventually for many of us to allow more healing and love to come in.

When we open our hearts more fully, all kinds of more nourishing things begin to happen. We think differently and draw in more positive events and people into our lives. We have more body, mind, and spirit energies that surge up. Our creative instincts improve and we communicate better. We can complete projects more easily, emotional and even physical healings happen more quickly, and our immune system improves – and on it goes.

Easy Heart Openings

> "What happens when people open their hearts?
> "They get better."
> – **Haruki Murakami**, **Norwegian Wood**

Think about what makes you feel happy, joyful, calm, peaceful, or just what makes you simply smile. Think about all your senses; smell, sight, hearing, feeling, etc. For example, I love the sight and smell of roses, lilacs, and carnations especially. I love babies, being by water, lying in the sun at a beach, the smell of the forest, hearing certain kinds of piano music, being with a good friend or family member, playing or watching a favorite sport, dancing, or just being outside.

As easy as this thinking sounds, as soon as you begin to think and then feel what brings you happiness, your heart being so connected with your spirit and sense of joy will automatically begin to open even more.

If you don' t already, place pictures around you of any of the things that bring feelings of being uplifted. We have pictures of our loved ones or places we love going to around us at home or at work because they are spirit lifters and heart mirrors for us to be reminded of the love that surrounds us and is always within us.

Quiet Focus Within

When possible, steal yourself away from overstimulation and noise to a place where you can be silent and hear your own inner voice.

- Take some deep breaths and just look into your heart and focus on it. Our heart's true nature is full of its own gentleness, kindness, compassion, and patience. The more open our heart can be, the more we can feel a caring and accepting connection to ourselves and to all of life that surrounds us. This is where we can consciously move our mind towards more peace and calm because the loving, compassionate energy will move from the heart and infuse our mind.
- Imagine: within your heart a beautiful red rose. As you focus on your heart, imagine this rose opening within your heart. Do this focus for a few seconds and you will feel more peaceful.
- Say to yourself, "I Am Peace, I Am Love, I Am Compassion." Know that this affirmation for you is true.

Extending Love and Compassion

As you see or pass by anyone, just say within yourself, "I send you love", "much love to you", "blessings to you", "peace for you" or, "may you be healed exactly as you need." Your silent or verbal word is your own powerful command to the larger loving energy grid to which we are connected. Your brief offering of compassion and caring will go directly to that person. You will find yourself smiling soon after with uplifted and lighter energy, because you will have sent them a positive strengthening.

We can do this for people, animals, or any and all of Earth's creatures. It also assists us in that same moment to open more to love. It adds to melting away any inner lingering resentment. On a more formal basis, we extend our love, compassion, and caring to others when we offer prayer on our own or in any of our spiritual groups or faith-based organizations.

If we can also choose to extend love and compassion, if only at a distance, or send a prayer to those that we are feeling resentful towards, when we feel are able to do that, then our energy can support their potential to open to healing.

It's more difficult to consider sending love to those we dislike and it is a more radical loving thing to do. When we send thoughts of love to those people in this way, we are sending out a higher energy and we act to defy the lower energy vibrations of fear and hatred. We assume, because we cannot ever expect to see a change in someone's behavior, that when we send this energy out nothing will ever happen.

We might not be aware of the power of a prayer or of the prayer offerings of others who are also sending their thoughts of love, light, and healing. At some point in time, our positive energy adding to the positive energy from others may well become the tipping point that begins to ignite a spark of conscious change and insight.

Gratitude

Encouraging ourselves towards a sense of gratitude or thankfulness is another way of opening and expanding our heart energy. Gratitude also increases our ability to receive more abundance. Do this by simply thinking of all the things for which you are grateful. When we do this, we are giving the Universe permission to bring us more of the things that make us thankful.

146

We are not focusing on our perceived lacking of anything in that instant.

For example, if you find a nickel or dime on your path, don't feel it's too small an amount to pick up – rather, do retrieve it and say, "thank you" – again expressing gratitude while at the same time opening to the Universe to provide you with more. When you express thankfulness, you also raise your vibration to a higher level.

Therefore, in any point in time – or when you go to sleep and upon awakening – simply say thank you for all the things, abundance, people, and situations that support you on your life path. Think of the comfort as well as the learnings that have been brought to you.

Music

We know that music has great impact on people as well as all animal and plant life. Before beginning any writing or healing session, I will put on a piece of piano, pan flute, harp, or guitar music, as are my preferences to open my heart, soften my mind and raise my energy. In fact, during the writing of my first book as well as this one, I consistently used Doug Volz's piano playing in the background as I wrote.

When I need to do housework, I put on something that makes me want to move and dance. We each have our own favorites but when it comes to what softens and calms us we tend to be drawn to musical tones that resonate with our hearts and gives our spirits a lift.

I believe our most natural balanced state is to be at peace. By opening our hearts, we begin to have an increased sense of being connected with nature, or at one with the energy that surrounds us.

In this realm of acceptance, our energy expands and becomes lighter. We begin to leave the former place of stress and constriction that lowers our vibration. Moving our vibration upwards expands the real strength and power in the attributes of love – compassion, kindness, empathy, and forgiveness.

David Hawkins in *Power vs. Force* (2012) says it well:

"Power is what makes you strong, while force makes you go weak. Love, compassion and forgiveness, which may be mistakenly seen by some as submissive, are in fact profoundly empowering." (p. 162)

Forgiveness

What does forgiveness mean? It means to consciously choose to let go and to find less value in continuously reliving a history where anger and hatred reside. *"It is letting go of the desire to hurt others or ourselves because of something that is already in the past"* (Jampolsky, G. 2007, p.17).

Letting go of resentments of any nature can be hard work if they've been there awhile. To forgive is to free ourselves emotionally and spiritually because it allows us to live more fully in the present moment with far more calmness. Forgiveness in some instances takes years to resolve depending on different factors.

I can say that depending on the impact of the emotional injury, forgiveness is generally not a one-time practice. It can be a frequent and necessary process if we find remnants of grudges that continue to be triggered. Those triggers will tell us that we are not finished releasing resentment, hurt, or a loss of some kind.

No matter how small the inner active hurt or grudge, it can still lower our energy because it will create an energy block, a sore, and it will keep returning to us to be healed. Sores have a way of festering when left unattended and can develop into more serious issues or even manifest as physical ailments.

There are also moments when we realize that even more than forgiving someone else, we need to stop being so angry at ourselves and accept and forgive ourselves for being caught in a situation that felt injurious to us, or where we felt we consciously made the wrong decision and got hurt by the result.

What I've found helpful in my own healing processes over time is to be able to come to a place where I can open and see the strengths and goodness in others, no matter what I feel has happened and to look with compassion in that they too have their own journey full of hazards, mistakes, and sometimes painful learning. They too have the same Universal source of energy within them and on that level, we all are connected, even if we don't wish to be. As part of my Reiki training, we do acknowledge the Divinity within all of us and this understanding connects us all throughout our human family.

Some people will wake up after a life-altering event and discover a kinder, more compassionate part of themselves that emerges. They then decide to pass on their learning. Others have a different journey to follow but can also be teachers for us. Their difficult and sometimes injurious behavior can move us to stand our ground with far more strength and backbone, playing a catalytic role in promoting our personal growth.

Remembering Our Innocence

Another thing we can do to help move us towards acceptance, forgiveness, and more peace is to remind ourselves of the innocent person that we all are inside, regardless of what has happened in our lives that may blocked us from time to time in achieving a fuller connection to our Creator.

Sometimes when we know of someone who has a really distasteful personality, or in a more extreme example, has committed some heinous act, we will search for some reason for it and ask, "What happened to them? Who or what kind of beliefs brought them to do that? What were they like as a child?" We recognize that something came into play that took them from a more natural state of innocence and wonder about the world.

If you go back in time to your childhood photos and follow your life path in pictures up through the ages, you will see your core innocence and the fact you were always curious to learn more about yourself in this world – or to at least be given the chance to find where you truly belong. You'll see that you still have the pureness of heart that loves the simple, joyful things in life. You can also see that same innocence you have reflected back to you in the unconditional love from animals, or from babies and children.

If we are at odds with anyone, we can also think of him or her in a state of innocence as a child. While that thought might never make you want to spend any further time with the individual, it can help dissolve some degree of resentment.

Forgiveness Exercise

Forgiveness does not always mean we will simply forget what happened, but it can mean that the incident or situation that we experienced as a painful one will not have the same negative power to hold us back or influence how we move our lives forward. The following mindfulness exercise is never to be felt as a strain, it is meant to be a gentle guide. It can be done as many times as you wish, and you can create your own exercises over time.

Breathe in and out slowly and ground yourself in the moment. Visualize a bubble of white light completely surrounding you – like an egg shape. This is your energy shield and no negative energy is able to penetrate it.

Only when you are ready, think of the person that you feel has created hurt or harm to you. See them sitting or standing before you. You may or may not fully understand the reason for the person's actions towards you, but you can tell this person:

I don't like what you did and I accept what has happened. I now choose to move forward in my life.
I accept you as you are and I forgive you for your actions.
I accept and forgive the situation; I let go of what happened.
I move on to greater strength.
I move on to greater wisdom.
I move on to greater love.
May you find healing you need with our Creator.
May you find peace within yourself.
May you find the love that resides within you.
May you be able to bring more love into this world.

Being released from resentment helps us to connect back to our hearts and have a greater sense of inner peace.

Staying Present in the Moment

Eckhart Tolle has written some wonderful books on being present. Try this experiment offered in Tolle's 1999 book *The Power of Now*:

"Close your eyes and say to yourself: 'I wonder what my next thought is going to be?'

Then become very alert and wait for your next thought. Be like a cat watching a mouse hole. What thought is going to come out of the mouse hole? Try it now."
"Well?" (p. 93)

Those who tried this exercise will likely comment that it took a while for a thought to arrive. Tolle remarks,

"As long as you are in a state of intense presence you are free of thought. You are still, yet highly alert. The instant your conscious attention sinks below a certain level, thought rushes in. The mental noise returns. The stillness is lost. You are back in time." (p. 94).

Being present does not feel like an easy thing to do most of the time, nor do we think of practicing this state of consciousness very often. Often, we find ourselves moving from one thought or one activity to another. We try to stay on top things as we attempt to slow down the momentum of any fears or challenges that are vying for our attention.

Tolle and others who extensively practice the art of meditation speak to the need to be grounded in our bodies to initiate a greater state of being present. The focus on deep breathing into our bodies is a key to being more present, calm, and relaxed (see chapter 3).

Managing Fear and Anxiety in the Moment

The fastest way I know of calming myself from moments of stress or anxiety is to breathe deeply. Just taking several deep breaths to calm your mind and body will work immediately. If need be, with each inhalation you can add these statements:

"I breathe in Strength, I breathe out Fear. I breathe in Courage, I breathe out Fear. I breathe in Calm, I breathe out Fear. I breathe in Love, I breathe out Fear."
"I am loved".

You can also tell yourself:
"I AM Kindness, I AM Empathy, I AM Compassion, I AM Strength, I AM eternal."

When you say these statements, you are connecting with your spiritual nature and you are aligning with what is spiritually known as the *I AM Presence* or what's also referred to as your Higher Self. If we can return for a time to affirm those strong qualities we have within us, we can help to rebalance and calm ourselves.

Self-care in Advanced Care Planning

I want to include advanced care planning in this writing because there is also an underlying fear that permeates many of our responses and decisions in life, a fear we'd rather not discuss much. It is fear of our own mortality.

Facing death by allowing for open discussion of our end-of-life transitions is an important part of how we need to care for ourselves and show caring for those close to us.

This area of self-care is a large area of discussion that lends itself to many informative steps involving issues related to decision-making for: personal health care issues, mental incapacity, financial management, palliative care, as well as wills and funeral arrangements. There are local, regional, and provincial legal and health care centers throughout Canada to assist in all ways in end-of-life preparations.

Resource Link in British Columbia:

Advance Care Planning/HealthLink BC
- https://www.healthlinkbc.ca/health-feature/advance-care-planning

Co-Creating What We Already Deserve

The idea that we are helping to co-create our lives involves how we use our energy in our thoughts, words, beliefs, and actions to manifest what we want to see unfold in our lives. Co-creation becomes a greater reality when we consider we are in an energy exchange with the same powerful Universal loving energy that surrounds us and runs throughout our world.

This idea of creating our lives as we go forward in linear time is not to suggest that if we are not where we think we should be that there is something inherently wrong. We begin our journeys in different degrees of privilege and circumstance and we have our own paths of spiritual learning.

This world can be unquestionably challenging at times. It does not serve us to judge ourselves in any way or to compare ourselves to others that appear to be far more successful. It helps us to be reflective in acknowledging our courage, strength and resiliency in the difficulties we have already overcome and to go forward from there.

What we can also do is take what we know about ourselves and see if we can make changes that feel initially doable. If we check into our daily self-talk and listen closely, we will hear where we are affirming ourselves, positively or negatively. All of those thoughts and feelings impact our self-esteem and energy levels and how we move ourselves towards what we want to see happen in our lives.

We might start out by thinking of having a better job, relationship, etc., but then we might catch ourselves thinking that maybe we aren't quite good enough to receive it or we don't really deserve it, or some other self-doubt. In that case, we might not take any action to shift us in the direction we really want to go.

If we want a chance to see changes in some of our outcomes, we can start with working on a shift of any false beliefs or thought patterns about our worthiness. We also need to be discerning about with whom we choose to invest our time. Those people who do not really have our best interests at heart and who are not genuinely interested in our success – their energy, influence and messages can be eroding.

The best action we can take is to maintain, as often as possible, a deeper, steadfast appreciation of who we are in our gifts, skills, and strengths and by continuing to express who we are, without unrealistic notions of perfection. *To truly believe and feel that we all deserve to receive the best that life has to offer is a powerful singular thought.*

If there are any areas of inner turmoil or resentment, this is where our focus needs to be to develop more inner peace. Co-creation doesn't just involve thinking and feeling what we want, it also involves using the information that's just been written regarding, *opening your heart, extending gratitude and compassion and working on acceptance and forgiveness for ourselves, and for others that we feel have harmed us.*

These areas all concern our own life experiences and in how we can develop control in developing meaning, understanding and strength in processing them. These are the areas that when more fully resolved eventually bring us a sense of inner peace and calm.

If our inner life can be more peaceful, it can also make the energy we put forward on our own behalf much stronger and more magnetizing. We feel more energized and begin to move more quickly in the direction we want it to go. We begin to see that we can create better circumstances for ourselves when we can feel and know more decisively, we truly deserve to have them.

There are other benefits. When we clear away more inner blocks like resentment, guilt, shame, blame and other things that lower our energy, we will find all of our senses come alive. We become more sensitively tuned in to ourselves and to all of nature. We hear and see all things more deeply. Our intuitive gifts become acute and we experience our life with more joy and lightness of heart.

Overall, it becomes essential that we love and care for ourselves as much as we can.

Three Guiding Questions

1) "How May I Best Serve?"

I have found this simple question to be particularly useful when looking at changes I want to manifest in my own career path. It is a question posed to one's higher self. It is a way to be guided towards my highest good in giving service to humanity, a service that allows me to fulfill my gifts and creative energies in a way that brings me happiness and meets my financial needs.

When we ask this question, it allows us to be guided to the best path without needlessly worrying about our ego's concern about how our choices may appear to others. We are perfectly open to receive the information that comes to us.

I learned to ask this question at various times in my life as I grew and changed in my occupational pursuits. It was provided to me from a spiritually reflective book called, *Teachings of Silver Birch* (2002).

The information reflects that when we are pursuing our soul's highest calling in whatever vocation or service offering at any point in time, whether it be simple or complex in nature, all of the service we give is important when we give and interact from the heart. Silver Birch relays:

"The power that is behind you is the power of the Great Spirit in all of life, the greatest force in the universe. That power must manifest and you can help it to bring its force into your world. It does not matter what you do – whether you raise one up, whether you give a word of encouragement, whether you serve in things of spirit or things of matter – as long as you serve and you are not weary of service, you are instruments of the Great Spirit." (p.196)

2. "What Would a Wise Woman/Man Do?"

This is another simple question to help anyone to quickly draw up our own deeper wisdom when facing challenging situations and we need clarity for the right path or action to take. In a moment of quiet, just ask and you may find the answer comes quickly.

3. Will My Action Show Respect for Myself?

Asking this question brings an immediate answer. If we say, "No, it doesn't show respect for myself," and we carry on with the action anyway, we may have an addiction or over-attachment something – a situation, person or substance in the works, or a poor boundary operating.

We may also be frightened for some reason to make the decision that is more respectful and/or, we are afraid to say no. For whatever reason we have brought the question to mind, if we don't get a clear answer, it is then our decision to talk to someone or get some assistance to get our clarity.

A Manifesting Process

If we believe, feel, visualize and affirm something we want often enough it will most likely manifest in some form. Some helpful guidelines for positive co-creation are:

- **Be very clear** about what you want, because you are giving the Universal energy a specific command. The Universe responds precisely and fastest when your mind is clear and decisive.
- **List the specific details** describing what you want, because as you study it once a day, you will impress your wishes on your deeper unconscious mind.
- **FEEL** what it is you want and how it feels to receive it.
- **Get a good mental visualization** of what you want.
- **Find a physical representation** of what you want via a picture or drawing or smaller replication that will add to the strength of your project.
- **Ensure that what you are seeking is aligned with your highest good,** does not harm you, anything, or anyone else. Let it be based on knowing you truly deserve the best that life has to offer.
- **Keep as silent** as possible about what you are doing in your creation so the energy can quietly build up inside you – creating a stronger magnetic pull from the energies that surround you.
- **Be truly ready and open to receive** what you want and visualize it happening.
- **Become present in your imagination** and affirm you have now received what you want (e.g. "I now have the job opportunity as a _____ and I feel great!")
- **Let it go!** Let your request go and continue on with your day. Take it easy knowing that all things come in the right time and the right way when we are ready to receive them. Some things can take years to arrive, but when they do, the timing makes sense to us in retrospect.
- **Act on or respond to any intuitive ideas, nudges or messages** from others that you receive. When you take a step forward, the universe will automatically illuminate the next step for you.

- **Try to remain patient** as things unfold – it's only the ego part of us that gets scared and overly demanding. Just tell it that everything's going in the right way. Go outside and play, then continue to listen to your intuitive, spirit self for next steps.
- **Love and care for yourself** as much as you can.

Know that the Universal energy that we are connected into is loving and supportive in nature and constantly works with us to help us achieve the successful outcome we deserve. This is one of the most important things to keep in mind. I have had moments of doubt as anyone does, when venturing into unfamiliar territory.

I have also experienced successful outcomes by also choosing to remind myself to trust in the nature of this loving, intelligent energy that lies within and around us - because it *will* continually attempt to provide for us in the ways we need in order for us to achieve. It will nudge us and give us subtle signals. We just need to take any small step that comes to mind towards our goal.

Affirmations for Health and Wellness

"Affirmations are our mental vitamins, providing the supplementary positive thoughts we need to balance the barrage of negative events and thoughts we experience daily."

— Tia Walker (with Peggi Speers)

I believe that positive affirmations are our own power statements and act like specific commandments to the Universal energies.

In essence, as spiritual beings they are our inherited right to proclaim – to use our word in the correct way to bring about positive change that can only do good for us and cannot harm anyone or any other sentient being. The following are some examples of daily affirmations to consider that can strengthen you:

- Every day in every way, I am getting healthier and stronger
- I am confident in my ability to manage all situations that come my way
- I eat healthy foods
- I develop habits that support a healthy lifestyle
- I am creative, intelligent, strong, and youthful
- I respect myself
- I am open to receiving all the abundance life has to offer
- I deserve to receive everything I need and that brings me happiness
- There is enough abundance for us all
- I practice gratitude daily
- I am patient
- I can stand up for what is important to me
- I have healthy boundaries
- I never give up
- I deal constructively with challenges
- I look for and find solutions
- I welcome any necessary help to assist me
- I am open to receive more love in my life
- I can do it!

Synchronicity

"Synchronicity is an ever present reality for those who have eyes to see."

– Carl Jung

Synchronicity is part of our co-creation and manifestation processes. As you proceed on your day, you'll notice the coincidences that come into your life to guide you in the way you want to go. These include those so-called chance encounters with people that give you guidance or information just when you need it, or when you get flashes of insight to contact someone who helps you. They can also be when you see words on a sign, books that come into your possession, images you see, or songs you happen to hear at the right time. These are all signals that you are on the right path.

This is the supportive, loving Universe communicating with you in ways to get your attention, letting you know you are heard and it's there to support and assist you. This is what being in the flow is about. It is essentially allowing yourself to put your effort forward in terms of using your imagination, visualization, and affirmations clearly, and then letting it all go and not pushing or forcing anything – just allowing yourself to gently feel the energies around you that are helping you.

This is the area of trusting that things will work out if you stay with it and don't get in your own way. Sometimes this process tests our patience, but it is a good thing, since most times we get impatient and forget that there is a degree of timing involved that we need to allow in receiving what we need or want.

Sometimes, there are other signals that we may begin to see, like repeating numbers. Numbers such as 111, 222, 333, 444's, etc. There are other repeating numerical sequences that I, as well as others have seen appearing around me far more frequently.

There are no coincidences here, as numbers represent universal vibrations in their energy patterns and it's up to us to figure out how to read the energy signals. If you talk to people about number sequences, you might find to your surprise that you have company for discussion.

Many people are noticing this phenomenon and some have attributed it to the increased connection to our higher selves. It can also mean we are more directly receiving the guidance of the Angelic realm, indicating there is more assistance being given at this time on Earth. There are books and websites that describe this phenomenon and writers like Doreen Virtue (2008) offers an introduction to the topic in her book referenced below. There are writers like Lorna Byrne, Kevin Basconi and many others available if you decide to search.

Other signals that I have always looked for during my life are with all forms of nature. I have received specific kinds of warnings or greetings of joy from birds such as crows, eagles, robins, owls, ravens, and songbirds. Other land or sea animals who suddenly appear, out of place and when least expected, usually hold meaning and provide thoughtful pause as a signal for me.

Overall, the Universe knows what kind of signals make sense to each of us in following our paths, and the more we choose to notice, the more often we will see them.

Resources for Co-creating, Affirming, and Manifesting

There are countless CDs, downloads from the Internet, and many excellent books that offer guidance for co-creating, manifesting, and developing your own affirmations. The following are some book offerings:

- Dyer, Wayne (2007) *Change Your Thoughts, Change Your Life*. Hay House Publishing
- Gawain, Shakti. (2002) *Creative Visualization*. Nataraj Publishing; Division of New World Library
- Hay, Louise. (1984) *You Can Heal Your Life*. Hay House Publishers,
- Hay, Louise. (1996) *Life*! Hay House Publishers, 1996
- Hicks, Esther and Jerry. (2004) *Ask and it is given*. Hay House Publishing
- Wilde, Stuart. (1987) *Affirmations*, by Dove International Inc. Taos, New Mexico, USA
- Wilde, Stuart. (1988) *The Quickening*. Hay House Inc.
- Virtue, D. (2008). *Angel Numbers, 101. The Meaning of 111, 123, 444, And Other Number Sequences*. Hay House.

Chapter 9
Self-Care Becomes Global Care

Every conscious act towards supporting our own self-care continues on as an active positive energy that ripples outward adding nourishing vitality throughout our homes and into our communities. The more we extend and build on the energy of love through kindness and compassion, the more it grows and has a positive influence on our Earth's environment.

Another aspect that evolves when we go forward in loving self-care is we become increasingly conscious of the ways and means we can responsibly harvest, replenish, and sustain our Earth. We become invested in knowing the Earth is also being given utmost regard in land and soil conservation practices to yield the highest quality of food.

We care more about the quantity, quality, and conservation reserves of our water. We are concerned about the air we breathe. If we consume animals or use animal by-products, we find out about the animal's well-being in their quality of life and their end of life. Some of us also transition away from animal consumption.

When we increase the focus on paying attention to the ways we show love and respect for ourselves, we also notice all manner of industries, services, and legislated governing bodies that provide for us. We want to know that they are accountable in upholding the sanctity of life by developing policies, practices, and procedures that contribute to our and the planet's well-being.

Moreover, as we continue to move and open our hearts and minds in this positive direction, many of us will experience our lives shifting in other ways. We will understand people with deeper and clearer perceptions and we will feel the cord of universal connectedness, even with those who may view life through a completely different lens.

We will also feel an even greater depth of caring for animals and all Earth life. This connection to animals will feel more profound as we embrace the fact that we are all sentient beings in our own unique physical, emotional, and spiritual senses. We will be able to look into the eyes of an animal, or even a small bird for example, and we will feel its soul. We will consider the creatures of the sea, like whales and dolphins, and we will realize these high-souled, cultural, and intelligent beings may instinctively have an awareness of who we are more than we realize, when we enter the waters of their home.

We will view an insect or a reptile that we once found uninteresting or even frightening and easily sense its innate intelligence. Our ability to more fully connect with creatures, plants, and all of Earth's life forms will become an ongoing source of respectful curiosity, learning and joy. We will begin to sense the remarkable intelligence and synchronistic beauty of our Earth.

The Earth is an Intelligent Being

When we spend time in nature we can feel that special energy all around us; energy we love and find spiritually rejuvenating. We can return to more of our own inner peace when we take in the healing energy the Earth gives.

Many of us reflect on this energy when we're at our office desks and we think about being by the ocean, or hiking – some place that takes us to our natural grounded sense of connection. When we spend time with Earth, many of us feel we are with a mother source. That experience would be true in a way because we contain the very elements of Earth. Our energy is connected to our Earth through our hearts and spiritual centers as well.

From an energetic and spiritual perspective, researchers like Robert Coon, who authored *Earth Chakras – The Definitive Guide* (2009), also recognize that our Earth is a living being that has its own life chakra energy system, just as we do. Coon states,

"The Earth is alive, with its own chakra and circulatory system. Great ley arteries transmit vitalizing forces around the

world through major sacred sites, advancing the evolution of all life." (http://earthchakras.org/Introduction.php).

Coon cites the seven main Earth chakra locations on the planet:

First Chakra (Root): Mount Shasta, California

This chakra is considered to be primal in generating Earth's life force prior to the life assuming biological form.

Second Chakra: Lake Titicada, Peru-Bolivia, and South America

This high elevation center's dual purpose has been to regulate new species on the Earth as well as Earth's major evolutionary advancements for life.

Third Chakra: Uluru-Kata Tjuta, Northern Territory, Australia

Enormous monolithic rock, also known as Ayers Rock and acts like the Earth's solar plexus. This rock acts to maintain, energize, and increase the health of all in the area.

Fourth Chakra: Glastonbury and Shaftesbury, England

These locations in England act like Earth's heart chakra and are thought to be the home of the Holy Grail. This high, spiritual vortex is purposeful in opening our hearts and raising the frequency of all life forms, as well as encouraging individuals globally towards more love and compassion.

Fifth Chakra: Great Pyramid, Mt Sinai, Mt. of Olives, and Middle East

This is considered to be the throat or voice of Earth's spirit, located perfectly central in the whole of our landmass. Its purpose is to align us with Earth's spirit to connect with her directly in order to understand her will for all dependent up on her.

Sixth Chakra: Aeon Activation Chakra

Like our pineal gland in the human brain that activates us to perceive energy and life more deeply, this 6th chakra is an activation center that helps humankind to perceive the other dimensions of our Earth and how we can participate in advancement of life in its many forms over longer periods.

Seventh Chakra: Mount Kailas, Tibet

The Crown Chakra, Mt. Kailas is the roof of the world. Considering the high spiritual teachings, the Tibetan people have brought to humankind, one can see a powerful energy that is meant to be instrumental in allowing the individual purpose and Earth's evolutionary purpose to be unified. This unification is dedicated to the overcoming of the sense of life decline and spiritual death, to the understanding of our eternal spiritual nature.

For more information, visit:

http://earthchakras.org/Locations.php

If we look at each of the chakra sites as laid out by Coon, and if we have had opportunity to travel to any of these main energy power centers, we will most likely feel that any of these centers have prompted deeper insights and changes for us. Many times, we are drawn to various places on this planet for that very reason; we are resonating an energy that begins to pull us to the very place we need to go to make that deeper connection with ourselves.

There are other key points on our planet that when we visit we tell ourselves, "I know this place", "I feel I have been here before", or "I feel I am home." When I lived in the Yukon Territory, spent time in parts of Egypt, England and the UK, and in Sedona, Arizona, I felt a strong spiritual connection to these locations. There are other places in the world that I long to travel to because instinctively I know they are areas that will enrich my soul.

Robert Coon is one of many authors that tell us there is so much more to our planet as an entire complex energy body than the knowledge of the Earth's chakras. There is far more information about the kinds of intelligent, interconnecting energy systems of our Earth that the reader can explore.

The Earth's Intelligence in Sacred Designs

One cannot help but take pause at the brilliance and beauty of Earth's specific designs found throughout our natural universe. I am referring to the geometric designs that not only reflect how our form as human beings is constructed, but are also part of the geometric matrix of the entire universe.

The drawing below of the ancient figure of the Flower of Life has been studied over thousands of years and is recognized mathematically as containing all the elements involved in creation of all matter, time, and space.

In his writings contained in *The Ancient Secret of The Flower of Life, Volume 1* (1998), Drunvalo Melchizedek relays the clarity he received regarding the energetic geometric meaning of the Flower of Life while at the ancient site at Abydos by stating,

"This design contains in its proportions, every single aspect of life there is. It contains every mathematical formula, law of physics, every harmony in music, and every biological life-form right down to your specific body. It contains every atom, every dimensional level, absolutely everything that's within wave form universes" (p. 29).

Figure 1. Flower of Life

I had the opportunity several years ago to travel to Egypt on a sacred spiritual journey in which we visited many powerful spiritual centers of Egypt's ancient origins.

In visiting Abydos, we came upon the same drawing of the Flower of Life as Melchizedek. The Egyptologist informed us, at the time, that this drawing in this particular location is thought to be one of the oldest in origin on the planet. The design of the Flower of Life was burned into the stone at Abydos and it was barely visible from the distance where I stood while photographing it and, unfortunately, it cannot be visually reproduced clearly enough to include in this writing.

Many of us will automatically recognize this design as is a symbol found in many worldwide religions as well as in our mathematical symbols. Mathematics is a universal language and the Flower of Life symbol is a part of mathematical sacred geometry. Geometry and mathematical ratios, harmonics, and proportions are also found in music, light, and cosmology (Melchizedek, 1998, p. 41).

Most of us studied geometry in our earlier school years with mathematical principles and applications when we looked at triangles, cubes, and circles. I'm sure we had no idea we were working with Earth's most sacred blueprints.

Melchizedek (1998) essentially purports throughout his writing that sacred geometry opens doors to higher consciousness when one begins to closely examine these ancient designs. This perspective actually began long ago with the Greeks who placed foundational value in their belief that:

"Geometry and numbers are sacred because they codify the hidden order behind creation. They are the instruments used to create the physical universe" (Skinner, 2006, p. 15).

In nature, geometric designs are abundant. Spirals are only one example of many and they can be easily found – in the horns of animals or in shells like the chambered nautilus in Figure 3. On a massive scale, we can view them in the giant galaxy in Figure 4, an example of our own spiral Milky Way galaxy. With both figures, there appears to be the same geometric logarithmic spiral formulae at play that is also fractal (Skinner, 2006, p. 58).

Figure 2.
Chambered Nautilus
(Clipart.com)

Figure 3
Spiral Galaxy
(Clipart.com)

These natural and consistently repeating geo-recursive designs also referred to as fractals. You can see many of them easily as they are all around us in leaves, pinecones, broccoli, ferns, and even shorelines when viewed from high above.

Some of the geometric replications also come through great works of art. In past centuries, the necessary study and geometric understanding, or geometry of perspective, was a necessary prerequisite for the production of great art and great architecture Skinner (2006, p. 89). That perspective is still true today of many art and architectural forms.

Many artists throughout time have been spiritually drawn to replicate nature through their meditations. Such is the case of those artists producing relatively precise geometric art forms – many primarily by freehand. In the creation of these designs as well as in viewing them, it allows any of us to access deeper parts of our consciousness and it can provide healing. Examples of sacred geometry are found in the inspirational sacred geometric mandala designs from two artists below.

Figure 4. Sacred
Geometric
Mandala
Meg MacQueen,
Holistic Health Coach

Figure 5. The Tree of
Cosmic Self-Knowledge
Claire Murgatroyd
(*clairemurgatroyd.com*)

"These mandalas are hand-drawn intuitively, and radiate a vortex of harmonizing energy; each one is "alive." Each is unique and created with pure intention and infused with energy. The design is natural and universal and connects with us on a cellular level. They radiate energy even when simply hanging on a wall and can support healing when used as a meditation tool. The act of drawing a mandala can also be a healing experience and a powerful tool of expression." (Meg MacQueen. www.megmacqueen.com)

With regard to her art designs Murgatroyd states, *"I use my art practice to develop and evolve a personal magical system. "The Tree of Cosmic Self-Knowledge" includes the symbolism of intertwining tree branches above and below the earth's horizon. The branches represent different time-lines of past life experiences. The semi-precious stone amber, fossilized resin from the sap of ancient trees, represents our inner spark and ancient connection to the universal source." (www.clariemurgatroyd.com)*

We can see the prevailing universal intelligence in these few but compelling examples of telluric designs through the creative connection and love expressed by artists. When we embrace Earth in a heart-sense way, our artistry flows through in beautiful synchronicity.

Earth's expressions of her creations are precise, intricate, delicate, and powerful in their scope beyond time and space. As we notice these shapes throughout our Earth and recognize the Being we are living upon, we are naturally deepened to want to ensure there is no harm created to the Earth or its inhabitants.

What Earth Needs

In 1992, US NASA astronaut Jack Lousma, on 1973 Skylab Space Station and as the president and chief executive officer at the time of the Centre for International Earth Science Information Network, wrote the following as part of his Preface in *Pathways of Understanding. The Interactions of Humanity and Global Environmental Change:*

"When looking back at Earth from space, we realize how much we care for this place, the place where our relationships, memories, hopes, dreams, and ambitions reside. We wish we could convey the wonder, the marvel, the awe of this exquisitely beautiful blue and white sphere, suspended in its sea of blackness, with its appearance of unity and tranquility. Seeing Earth from space is a powerful, expansive experience that often makes us impatient with the relative pettiness that so often preoccupies and confounds us in more traditional surroundings.

This experience also makes us realize that Earth itself is a kind of spacecraft, and we are all astronauts upon it, hurtling along at amazing speed. Just as the inhabitants of a spacecraft must conserve supplies, keep their ship clean and strive to work together in harmony, we must do the same on Spacecraft Earth. If we are to enjoy a safe and successful mission, we must use our resources wisely, be good stewards of our environment and strive to improve our relationships." (Page 2; par.3)

What our Earth needs is what we need – that is respect, care, protection, and support to flourish and evolve. The Earth responds in various ways to our human activities as she does to other life forms. We have impact on the Earth and the Earth has direct impact on us.

As a living, sentient being that is made up of countless interrelated bio-diverse ecological systems, the Earth has a kind of conscious awareness of our collective energies where we gather in our communities. As our conscious awareness is increasing, we are also uplifting many parts of our world's ecological systems with improved environmentally sound replenishing practices.

Unfortunately, there is still a high degree of imbalance of our planet's environment that can render negative results for all of life, unless we cooperatively and globally forge a clear and persistent path for Earth's recovery. Although restorative efforts are being made, more needs to happen.

Still, we are on a trajectory to continue to participate in some significant Earth changes already underway. These changes in the magnitude and destructiveness of hurricanes, tornados, flooding, earthquakes, massive fires, frigid temperatures with loss of human and animal life and habitat have already caused shock, trauma, and hardship for millions.

There is much analysis regarding Earth's changes. One interpretation of our Earth's shifting activity is that there is a form of re-balancing and cleansing occurring. This may be as a result of Earth's natural life cycle shifts that may in part, contribute to global warming, while it also reacts to the impact of myriad resource extractions and all forms of water, soil and atmospheric pollutants.

While we can certainly interpret Earth changes in different ways, at minimum, these kinds of extreme global activities provide us with a loud wake-up call for more action to protect Earth and to prepare and protect ourselves as we adjust and live though the sudden ongoing and potentially catastrophic changes.

As I write this passage, I am fully aware that I am living in an earthquake zone on the west coast of British Columbia and that I am continuing to prepare as much as one can, for any sudden Earth changes.

Below is a website link to a short informative video of the possibility of how Earth's changes might look over the next 25 years as presented by Upworthy (Dec. 11, 2013, Mischa Reuben):

The Earth's Next 100 Years, Visualized - Upworthy
www.upworthy.com/the-future-of-the-earth-s-next-100-
years-visualized

In December 2015, world leaders became galvanized around global warming issues and from that endeavor the Paris Agreement on climate action was initially adopted by 195 countries. With differing and changing political perceptions of what this global change initiative can mean economically or otherwise, some countries over time may not wish to carry through in their full commitment to this global agreement. However, this legally binding global climate agreement was the first of its kind in human history.

There are significant key features of this agreement, but the main action plan is intended to limit global warming to well below 2 degrees Centigrade and achieve zero-net emission by the second half of the 21st century to avoid further dangerous climate changes. (Paris Agreement/Climate Action.

http://ec.europa.eu/clima/policies/international/negotiations/paris_en)

We know that although the challenges our global community is facing are serious, each one of us can make a difference in contributing to our Earth's replenishment. There appears to be greater public and political will being harnessed that will allow us clarity in the steps we all can take.

All Systems Are Changing

Along with Earth's changes, there are brilliant and exciting medical discoveries, technological advances, and environmental achievements that are instrumental in improving our lives and the planet's health. There are other changes in process as well that are extremely difficult and they are part of our extraordinary evolution at this particular time in history.

Life Affirming Feminine Energy

What we are also seeing is a resurgence of consciousness of the sacredness and necessity of feminine energy – that being the energy that is loving, life affirming and is contained in the core of all men and women. Although women have been in positions of power and influence throughout human history, the patriarchal energies and institutions that have emerged over time have generally repressed and oppressed the feminine energy within males and females.

This global shift in the rise of life-honoring energy will continue in direct response to patriarchal forms as we move away from severe oppressive imbalances such as wars, poverty, illness and starvation on this planet. The various socio-economic and political institutions that have exerted a negative consolidation of power over many parts of our world's communities are all coming to light.

It seems like the very heart of humanity is pressing forward with an ardent groundswell of expression to demand we live in peaceful co-existence and that there be real life-honoring and sustaining system changes. This passionate call from our world's citizens is an additional demand for equality for all and is being created by our own deeper love and self-regard. There is an abiding realization that we all are in fact, the rightful heirs of the abundance of this world. These changes can and will occur as the light of truth continues to shine on all outmoded systems that do not affirm humanity and all Earth life.

From my healer's perspective, this epoch is akin to a large-scale extraordinary and painful uprooting process of toxic forms with an eventual outcome of positive healing for humanity and our planet. This healing can happen when we assert the more heart-centered loving parts of our own nature; when we individually and collectively give voice and act on behalf of the caring and concern we have for ourselves, each other and this planet.

These are the very times that many sensed were coming but may not have known how quickly or in what exact form they'd manifest. The pace of changes, positive or negative, seems to be accelerating. As many have been watching, studying, and reading about the transformative time that's now upon humanity and the Earth, there seem to be others who are not as aware of this extraordinary time of change.

A compelling 2013 book, *Collapsing Consciously: Transformative Truths for Turbulent Times* by Carolyn Baker, a long-time American social activist, calls people out on her perception of a collective denial about systems' changes that may be moving towards a potential collapse. Baker provides warning signals and speaks to her concern about individuals' lack of preparedness to deal with it. Her book is an interesting and sobering read.

Whomever presents information that we may agree with or not, it's important to stay as positive and supportive to ourselves and each other as possible. It's good to be discerning about what is truly happening around us and to be aware of any information coming our way to give us needed direction. Wherever we happen to be, the Earth will always be sending us signals and, just as animals listen and follow, we also need to try and listen with our own GPS – our inner intuition. It will always help to guide our steps.

Listening to the Indigenous Peoples

"The Earth changes are here. I am glad they are. They're necessary for the survival of the planet. This is what we Indians were told long ago and what Spirit tells us today. These changes are a time of cleansing. Right now, the Earth is like a great big shaggy dog and humans are like flees in its hair. When the dog starts shaking we get very worried, as well we should.

*The reason the Earth changes are happening, and will continue to happen, is because many humans are not yet willing to make necessary changes in themselves and their actions, which could prevent them. They are not willing to stop polluting and to start moving in a sacred manner. They will not stop throwing their garbage all over the planet." (*Sun Bear, Wabun Wind, 1992, *p. 51).*

Indigenous peoples have watched and warned us of what we need to consider with these forthcoming changes. As caretakers of the Earth, Indigenous peoples have long held the sacred and holistic belief that there is an intimate connection between the health of the Earth and the health of the person.

This means in all bio-diverse ways the Earth must be honored and protected from air, water, and soil pollutants. The Earth must be preserved in a manner that respects healthy resource development and conservation practices that preserve the integrity of all life forms. Earth does not exist simply for the taking. Whatever is needed, only that amount should be removed or extracted in a way that does not harm the Earth's elements or her ability to be replenished, all to ensure future generations can also be fully nourished.

Unfortunately, we know that around the world Indigenous people's historical holistic beliefs and practices have not been followed in the advent of the global industrialization processes affecting trade, culture, environment, and technology.

As all peoples and life forms on the planet are now being exposed to untold numbers of contaminants and pollutants, it becomes vital that we listen to the Indigenous peoples' leadership and their ability to provide a necessary perspective and the cooperative stewardship we need. With their involvement in developing respectful policies and sound methods of eco-systemic resource and conservation management we will, step by step, gain ground in upholding Earth's and humanity's recovery.

Send Healing Thoughts to Earth

One of the many things we can do for our planet besides being mindful of important go-green environmental strategies is to send our thoughts of love and healing to Earth. As I mentioned in an earlier chapter, we know that thoughts of love and gratitude have a very positive energetic impact on human, animal, and even plant bodies.

We can also send the same kinds of thoughts to all parts of our Earth as a simple blessing. For example, when I walk by the ocean, I send the water thoughts of love and gratitude. I just say, "I bless the waters with love and thank you." I send similar thoughts when I walk near the forest, or by rock places, or any area that has Earth's growth. I practice sending love and healing to this entire planet and to all the animals and plant life. I send these blessings to Earth because again, our thoughts are energy and we can have a cumulative, positive impact on all matter when we send it love and healing. It is a simple thing to do.

We can also visualize the waters and the air being clean and pure and Earth life being restored. Thinking the positive and visualizing how we want our planet to look in wellness will help in the restorative process. Send Earth your love and gratitude as you can remember, it will all help.

Our Way Through with Love

"The greatest power that a human possesses is the power of pure love."

— Debasish Mridha

Globally, we are all likely feeling a shift occurring to some extent, even if it's not fully in our conscious awareness. It seems we are in the process of waking up and opening our hearts and minds to the reality that we can eventually transcend to a more loving race of beings – beings that we actually are at our core. I feel that most of humanity has an inner knowledge, spoken or otherwise, of the power of the human heart to help transform us and this planet on every level.

We are realizing this awareness as we connect with like-minded souls across international communities to promote this transformation. This is a way that humanity can both join with our living Earth and work cooperatively to metamorphose from the old to the new. We can move away from any archaic disempowering systems that continue to enslave citizens and exploit Earth's resources, to one where we govern our lives by embracing the powerful attributes of love, peace, and respect for the sacredness of all life.

There is strong combativeness in this change process now underway, and we can already see these conflicts occurring violently in old governing orders and institutions throughout the world that are not ready to give up power and control over masses of people.

There are practical issues we will need to keep in mind wherever we are on this planet to ensure we are as prepared as possible to get through the Earth's and all other systems' dramatic shifts. There will be the obvious need to be practical in all of our living preparations in taking stock of essential survival needs in terms of finances, nutrition, medical services, housing, and connecting with others through a sense of community and friendship.

We can still go forward where we are and use our energies wisely for ourselves, in our work, and in the care of our families and community of loved ones. We can continue to stand up for Earth's creature kingdoms that need our help to survive in the water, on land, and in the sky. We can still embrace our creative gifts, skills, talents, and listen to our heart's yearnings to follow and co-create a joyful path.

Emotionally and spiritually the attributes of love such as, empathy, compassion, and forgiveness are some of the key conscious practices that have carried me on my life's journey, kept me safer, and brought me healing and more happiness. These are also the mindful spiritual and emotional states I focus on if I am thrown off course from any sudden change or difficult situation. The energy of Love is ultimately an expansive and stabilizing force.

Beginning with our ability to focus on our self-care we can also use these same attributes of love and compassion to go forward in our lives with more strength and resilience, as we join globally to help carry us through the magnitude of changes that will affect every one of us in time.

As we choose to intentionally express our inherent loving natures we will tap into our greatest source of strength – the strength of our hearts and spirits. From here we have the capacity to affect enormous positive changes for ourselves and for this entire planet.

References

- American Psychological Association. (2016) *The Road to Resilience.*
http://www.apa.org/helpcenter/road-resilience.aspx
- Baker, C. (2013) *Collapsing Consciously, Transformative Truths for Turbulant Times.* North Atlantic Books. Berkley, California.
- Barrett, S. PhD. (2013) *Secrets of Your Cells. Discovering Your Body's Inner Intelligence.* Sounds True Inc. Boulder, CO.
- Bartlett, R, (2007) *Matrix Energetics.* Atria Paperback. New York, NY, a division of Simon and Schuster, Inc. and Beyond Words Publishing Hillsboro, Oregon, a division of Simon and Schuster Inc.
- Bayliss, C.R., Bishop, N. L., Fowler, RC "Pineal gland calcification and the defective sense of direction." British Medical Journal. Volume 291, p 21-28 December 1985.
(https://www.ncbi.nlm.nih.gov/pmc/articles/PMC1419179/
pdf/bmjcred00479-0018.pdf)
- Beaudoin, Luc (2017). mysleepapp.com. Global News. http://globalnews.ca/news/3423143/b-c-professors-sleep-technique-gets-attention-from-oprah/
- Berry, Thomas. (1988) *The Dream of the Earth.* Sierra Club Books, San Francisco.
- Bittman, Barry, Dr. *Group Drumming and Neuroendocrine-Immune parameters Alternative Therapies,* January, 2001, Vol. 7, No. 1, p. 38-47)
http://drumsofhumanity.org/wp-content/uploads/2012/01/Immune-System-Study.pdf

- Black, Jan and Enns, Greg. (1997) *Better Boundaries. Owning and Treasuring Your Life.* New Harbinger Publishers. Oakland, CA.

- Braden, Gregg, (2014, 2015) *Resilience From the Heart. The Power to Thrive in Life's Extremes* Hay House, CA.

- Bridges, William, PhD. *Managing Transitions. Making the Most Of Change.* William Bridges and Associates, Inc. (2009) Perseus Books Group, Philadelphia, PA (p. 99).

- Burney, Diana. (2009) *Spiritual Clearings. Sacred Practices to Release Negative Energy and Harmonize Your life.* North Atlantic books. Berkley, CA:

- Canada Safety Council. Canadasafetycouncil.org https://canadasafetycouncil.org/safety-canada-online/article/driver-fatigue-falling-asleep-wheel. online/issue/vol-liii-no-2-april-2009

- Canadian Sleep Review, *Current Issues, Attitudes and Advice to Canadians.* Developed in consultation with the Canadian Sleep Review Panel with support from Dairy Farmers of Canada. May 2016

- Chakra-Anatomy.com. 2016

- Chambers, Lin, Dr., NASA, *What Wave Length Goes With What Colour?*
www.science-edu.larc.nasa.gov. 07.22.2016.

- Chiasson, Ann Marie (2013) *Energy Healing. The Essentials of Self-Care.* Sounds True, Inc: Boulder, CO:

- Cichoke, Anthony J. (2001) *Secrets of Native American Herbal Remedies A Comprehensive Guide to the Native American Tradition of Using Herbs and the Mind/body/spirit Connection for Improving Health and Well-being.* Penguin Publishers.

- Chopra, Deepak, M.D. and Tanzi, Rudolph E., Ph.D. (2012) *Super Brain. Unleashing The Explosive Power of Your Mind To Maximize Health, Happiness, And Spiritual Well-Being.* Harmony Books, imprint of Crown Publishing Group, Div. of Random House, LLC, New York (p.97)

- Cichoke, Anthony J., (2001) *Secrets of Native American Herbal Remedies.* Avery

- Coon, Robert, (2009) *Earth Chakras, The Definitive Guide.* Lulu Press, Raleigh, North Carolina
- Coon, Robert (1967-2017)
http://earthchakras.org/Books.php
- Coon, Robert (1967-2017)
http://earthchakras.org/Locations.php
- Cooper, Diana. (2007) *Angel Answers.* Findhorn Press, Scotland, UK.
- Dangeli, Jevon. *Bio-Communication.* 2007-2017
- Doidge, Norman (2007) *The Brain That Changes Itself, Stories of Personal Triumph from the Frontiers of Brain Science.* Penguin Books
- Duck, J. D. (1993) *Managing the Change: The Art of Balancing*
- https://hbr.org/1993/11/managing-change-the-art-of-balancing, November-December Issue, 1993. par. 24)
- Dyer, W. (2007) *Change Your Thoughts, Change Your life.* Hay House Publishing
- Earthsky.org.teamelinorimster).
- Eleanor Imster *in* Earth, Science Wire. January 8, 2016.
- English/Oxford Dictionary.
www.Englishoxforddictionaries.com
- *First Nations Traditional Foods Fact Sheets. (First Nations Health Authority: fnha.ca. 2016) http://www.fnha.ca/wellnessContent/Wellness/Traditional_Food_Facts_Sheets.pdf*
- Fosar, Grazyna and Bludorf, Franz, article: *Scientists Prove DNA Can Be Reprogrammed by Words and Frequencies,* originally taken from the book *"Vernetzie Intelligenz (PDF) http://wakeup-world.com/2011/07/12/scientist-prove-dna-can-be-reprogrammed-by-words-frequencies/*
- Frost, Robert. (1914) *Mending Wall*, Collection of poems in North of Boston. Publisher, David Nutt
- Gagliano, Monica, Dr. *The Science of Plant Behaviour and Consciousness.* http://www.monicagagliano.com
- Gangsei, D., PhD. (2011) *Vicarious Trauma, Vicarious Resilience and Self-Care.* (PDF)
http://www.healtorture.org/.

- Gawain, Shakti, (2002) *Creative Visualization.* Nataraj Publishing; Division of New World Library,
- Geiger, John. (2013) *The Angel Effect.* Weinstein Books Publisher
- Gerber, Richard, M.D. *Vibrational Medicine.* The #1 Handbook of Subtle-Energy Therapies. (2001) Bear & Company, Rochester, Vermont, Third Edition
- Graham, Linda, (2013) MFT, *Bouncing Back, Rewiring Your Brain for Maximum Resilience and Well-Being.* New World Library, Novato, CA
- Halcrow, Barbara. (2011) *Spiritual Intelligence. How Your Spirit Will Lead You to Health, Happiness and Success.* Expert Author Publishing
- Hall, Judith. (2003) *The Crystal Bible.* Godsfield Press, division of Octopus Publishing Group, Ltd. Great Britain
- Halpern, Seven. *Chakra Suite.* Halpern Inner Peace Music. www.StevenHalpern.com
- Hawkins, David R. M.D., PhD. (1995, 1998, 2004, 2012) *Power vs Force, The Hidden Determinant of Human Behavior.* Author's Official Authoritative Edition. Hay House, CA
- Hay, Louise. (1984) *You Can Heal Your Life.* Hay House Inc.
- Hay, Louise. (1996) *Life*! Hay House Publishers
- Health Canada. *A Statistical Report On The Health of First Nations In Canada: Determinants of Health,* 2006-2010 (2014, p. 48).
  http://health.chiefs-of-ontario.org/sites/default/files/attachments/Determinants%20of%20Health%202006-2010-EN-FINAL.pdf
- Hensrud, D., M.D. *Is too little sleep a cause of weight gain?* (2015) In Sleep and weight gain: what's the connection? www.mayoclinic.org/healthy.../sleep-and-weight-gain/faq-200581.
- Hicks, Esther and Jerry. (2004) *Ask and It Is Given. Learning to Manifest Your Desires.* Carlsbad, CA, New Deli, Hay House, Inc

180

- Hoberman Levine, Barbara. (1991) *Your Body Believes Every Word You Say.* Santa Rosa, CA, Aslan Publishing
- Hornstein, H. (2008) *Using a Change Management Approach to Implement Programs.*
  http://iveybusinessjournal.com/publication/using-a-change-management-approach-to-implement-it-programs/. January/February Issue, 2008, par. 11)
- Jampolsky, Gerald C, M.D. (1999, 2007) *Forgiveness, The Greatest Healer Of All.* Atira Paperback, NY, NY; Beyond Words, Hillsboro, Oregon,
- Johnson, David, *Do different colours affect your mood?* Colours, Meanings and Moods. Colour Psychology 2000-2016.
  http://www.infoplease.com/spot/colors1.html
- Kotter, J. *Leading Change, Why transformational Efforts Fail,* In Harvard Buisiness Review, January 2007, (p.4) https://www.alaska.edu/files/pres/Leading-Change.pdf
- Kuthumi quote, from Milanovich, Dr. Norma and McCune, Dr. Shirley. (1996) *The Light Shall Set You Free.* Athena Publishing, Kalispell, MT. 4th Edition
- Levitin, Daniel, Chandra, Mona Lisa,*"Trends in Cognitive Science, (*2013, Vol. 17, No. 4.) *The neurochemistry of music. Journal Department of Psychology, McGill University, Montreal, Quebec, QC H3A 1B1, Canada*
  https://daniellevitin.com/levitinlab/articles/2013-TICS_1180.pdf
- Linden, Anne. (2008) *Boundaries in Human Relationships: How to Be Separated and Connected. Crown House Publishing Ltd. and Crown House Publishing Company LLC., CT*
  http://www.goodreads.com/quotes/tag/boundaries?page=2
- Lipton, Bruce, H, Ph.D. (2015) *The Biology of Belief. Unleashing the Power of Consciousness, Matter and Miracles.* Hay House, CA
- Lewis C.S., (1960) *The Four Loves.* Cox & Wyman Ltd., Fakenham for the publishers Geoffrey Bles Ltd. 52 Doughty Street, London WC

- London Health Sciences Centre; (16. 12. 2009) *Horizontal Hostility, Dealing With Difficult Situations In the Workplace;* Presentation to Preadmission Clinic Staff, Victoria Hospital, LHSC.
(http://www.opana.org/conference/presentations/2010-HORIZONTAL_HOSTILITY-Liz_Burke.pdf)
- Lindenfield, G. (2016) *Assertive Bill of Rights.* (http://www.londonstressmanagement.com/client_dow nloads/Assertive%20Bill%20of%20Rights.pdf)
- Lousma, Jack (1992) Preface in *Pathways of Understanding. The Interactions of Humanity and Global Environmental Change.* Centre for International Earth Science Information Network. University Centre, MI
(https://www.ciesin.columbia.edu/documents/CIESIN1 992PathwaysofUnderstanding_sm.pdf)
- Luke, Jennifer, School of Biological Sciences, University of Surrey, Guilford, UK, *Department of Obstetrics and Gynaecology, The Royal London Hospital*, published article, *Fluoride Deposition in the Human Pineal Gland;* in the International Center For Nutritional Research Inc., 2001, S Kargal, AG, Basal
(http://www.icnr.com/articles/fluoride-deposition.html)
- Ma'ati Smith, Dr. Jane, C.HyP., Msc.D., *Chakra Healing Sounds,*
http://balance.chakrahealingsounds.com/the-7-chakras
- MacLean, Kenneth, James, Michael. *The Vibrational Universe: Harnessing the Power of Thought to Consciously Create Your Life.* (2006) Book #1 in The Potential Consciousness Series. Baker and Taylor, Ingram Book Group, New Leaf Distributing, Loving Healing Press
- Manning, B. and Bennett, R. (2002) *Abba's Child; The Cry of the Heart for Intimate Belonging.* NavPress Publishing Group
http://www.goodreads.com/work/quotes/513762
- Markowitz, D. (2013) *Self-Care for the Self-Aware. A Guide for Highly Sensitive People, Empaths, Intuitives, and Healers.* Balboa Press. Bloomington. IN

- (Marques, J., Dhiman, S., King, D., (2007) *Spirituality in the Workplace. What It Is, Why It Matters, How to Make It Work For You.* Personhood Press, Fawnskin, CA (p. 133)

- Martinex-Conde, Susana, Machknik, Stephen L *How the Colour Red Influences Our Behaviour.* Scientific America, Behaviour and Society, 01.11, 2014); https://www.scientificamerican.com/.../how-the-color-red-influences-our-...

- Mate, Gabor. (2012) *When The Body Says No: The Cost of Hidden Stress.* Published by Vintage Canada, Division of Random House (p. xi)

- Mathieu, F. (2007) *Running on Empty: Compassion fatigue in Health Professional*
http://www.compassionfatigue.org/pages/RunningOnEmpty.pdf

- Mathieu, F. *"Compassion Fatigue What you don't know will hurt you."* This Changed My Practice (UBC, CPD) University of British Columbia. http://thischanged my practice/com/compassion-fatigue/

- McKay, Matthew, Ph.D., Davis, Martha, Ph.D., Fanning, Patrick. *Messages. The Communications Skills Book.* Third Edition. New Harbinger Publishers. Oakland, CA. 2009.

- Mcnally. Jess. *Earth's Most Stunning Natural Fractal Patterns.* Science. 09.10.10).
https://www.wired.com/author/j_mcnally

- Meichenbaum, D. & Research Director of The Melissa Institute for Violence Prevention and Treatment of Victims of Violence Miami, Florida. *SELF-CARE FOR TRAUMA PSYCHOTHERAPISTS AND CAREGIVERS: INDIVIDUAL, SOCIAL AND ORGANIZATIONAL INTERVENTIONS*
https://www.melissainstitute.org/documents/Meichenbaum_SelfCare_11thconf.pdf

- Melchizedek, Drunvalo. (1998) The Ancient Secret Of The Flower Of Life. Volume 1, by Clear Light Trust, Light Technology Publishing, Flagstaff, AZ

- Milanovich, Dr. Norma J. and McCune, Dr. Shirley. (1996) *The Light Shall Set You Free.* Athena Publishing, Kalispell, MT. 4th Edition
- Millman, Dan. (1980, 1984, New Edition, 2000) *Way of the Peaceful Warrior.* H.J. Kramer Book, Tiburon, California and published in joint venture with New World Library, Novato, California
- Mridha, D. quote from Goodreads

http://www.goodreads.com/author/show/7441013.Debasish _Mridha

- Moerman, Daniel. (1998) *Native American Ethnobotany* (Timber Press; online

http://www.herbmed.org/links.html

- Morgan, Nick. *Do You Have Change Fatigue?* Working Knowledge, HBS. 10.Sept.2001.

http://hbswk.hbs.edu/item/do-you-have-change-fatigue

- Moskowitz, Clara, *Fact or Fiction? Energy Can Neither Be Created Nor Destroyed.* In Scientific American. Scientific American, a Division of Nature America, Inc. Aug. 5, 2014
- Murakami, Haruki. (2000) *Norwegian Wood.* Vintage International Original
- Myss, Carolyn, PH.D. (1996) *Anatomy of the Spirit.* Harmony Books, Division of Random House. New York
- National Institute of General Medical Sciences. *Circadian Rhythm Fact Sheet, 04.06.2016*

https://www.nigms.nih.gov/Education/Pages/Factsheet_Cir cadianRhythms.asp

- The National Collaborating Centre for Aboriginal Health (NCCAH

http://www.nccah- ccnsa.ca/Publications/Lists/Publications/Attachments/ 46/health_inequalities_EN_web.pdf)

- Paris Agreement. Paris Agreement/Climate Action. http://ec.europa.eu/clima/policies/international/negotiat ions/paris_en)
- Pearce, Eiluned and Launay, Jacques, The *Ice-breaker Effect: Singing mediates fast social bonding,* are

published in journal *Royal Society Open Science* on 28 October: doi: 10.1098/rsos.150221.

- Pert. C. Dr. (2008-2016) *"Where Do You Store Your Emotions?"* The Institute of Medicine. *"*
http://candacepert.com/where-do-you-store-your-emotions/

- Povah, L. (2011) *Drum Circle Program for Eating Disorders*. Saint Paul's Hospital, Vancouver, BC.
http://drummingandhealth.com/wp-content/uploads/2012/07/Research-Study-Results-Drum-Circle-Program-2011.pdf

- Price, J. R. (1981, 1987) *The Superbeings. The Superselling Guide to Finding Your Higher Self. A* Fawcett Crest Book, Published by Ballantine Book

- Priest, S. & Gass, M. *An Examination of "problem-solving" versus "solution –focused in a corporate setting.* In Association for Experimental Education. May 1997, Vol. 20, No. 1; pp 34-37).
http://simonpriest.altervista.org/DOWNLOADS/ExaminationPSvSFFacilitation.pdf

- Prophet, E.C. (1997) *The Violet Flame to Heal Body, Mind and Soul*. Summit Publications, Inc.

- Prosci: *5 Tips for: Addressing Change Saturation. Change Management Tutorial. (1996-2014)*
http://www.change-management.com/tutorial-5-tips-saturation)

- Prosci. (1996-2014) *Change Saturation White Paper.*

- http://www.change-management.com/tutorial-saturation-white-paper.htm (par. 4)

- *Public Health Agency of Canada. Population Health. What Determines Health? Key Determinants.*
http://www.phac-aspc.gc.ca/ph-sp/determinants/index-eng.php#key_determinants

- Ray, A. (2110, 2015) Mindfulness: Living in the Moment – Living in the Breath. Inner Light Publishers.

- Reading, C, Ph.D., and Wien, F., Ph.D. (2009, 2013) *Health Inequalities And Social Determinants Of Aboriginal Peoples' Health,* in National Collaborating Centre For Aboriginal Health, University of Northern British Columbia, Prince George, BC

- Rendel, P. (1990) Understanding THE CHAKRAS, *Discovering and using the energy of your seven vital force centres.* Aquarian Press, Thorsons Publishing Group, Wellingborough, North Hamptonshire, England.
- Rome, D. I. (2014) *Your Body Knows The Answer, Using Your Felt Sense to Solve Problems, Affect Change and Liberate Creativity.* Shambhala Publications, Inc: Boston, MA
- Shiv, Vandana, M.D., (2014) *Golden Rice: Myth, Not Miracle.*
(http://gmwatch.org/index.php/news/archive/2014/15250-golden-rice-myth-not-miracle)
- Siegal, B. (*1989) Love, The Healer, in Carlson, Richard, Phd and Shield, Benjamin. Ed. Healers on Healing. Los Angeles; St. Martin's Press, NY*
- Silver Birch Series, *Teachings of Silver Birch (*1998) Edited by Austen, A.W. Spiritual Truth Foundation, Booksprint Printers, GB,
- Skinner, S. (2006) *Sacred Geometry. Deciphering the Code.* Sterling Publishing Co. Ink. New York, NY
- Speers, P., and Walker, T. (2013) *The Inspired Caregiver: Finding Joy While Caring for Those You Love.* Flowspirations, LlC, Monterey, CA
- Sun Bear with Wabun Wind. *Black Dawn* (1992*) Bright Day, Indian Prophecies for the Millennium that Reveal the Fate of the Earth.* Fireside, Simon and Schuster Building, New York, New York.
- The Australian. Editorial, *Europe's Compassion Fatigue.* (September 17, 2015) theAustralian.com.au.
http://www.theaustralian.com.au/opinion/editorials/europes-compassion-fatigue/
- The Self Help Alliance, University of Alberta. *Building Better Boundaries.*
https://www.ualberta.ca/medicine/departments/anethesology-pain-medicine/staff-well-being/e44e46425a004562b7e54068d56fb62e.ashx
- Tucker, Dr. Jim, and Stevenson, Ian. (2005, 2008) *"Life Before Life: A Scientific Investigation of Children's*

Memories of Previous Lives. St. Martin's Griffin, New York

- Turner, Dawn-Marie, Dr., (2015) *Launch, Lead, Live. The executive's guide to preventing resistance & succeeding with organizational change.* Your Nickel's Worth Publishing. Regina, SK
- Turner, Dawn-Marie
- http://thinktransition.com/articles/change-fatigue-is-your-organization-too-tired-to-change/
- Turtle Island Native Network: Healing and Wellness http://www.turtleisland.org/healing/healing-wellness.htm
- Upworthy. *The Earth's Next 100 Years, Visualized - Upworthy* (Dec. 11, 2013, Mischa Reuben) *www.upworthy.com/the-future-of-the-earth-s-next-100-years-visualized*
- Vaag, Jonas; Saksvik, Per Øystein; Theorell, Töres; Skillingstad, Trond, and Bjerkeset, Ottar. *"The Sound of Well-being- choir singing as an intervention to improve well-being among employees in two Norwegian county hospitals",* in *"Singing Improves Health and Work Environment"* (in Science Nordic, Nov. 12. 2012)
- Vancouver Coastal Health (2015) *Respectful Workplace Program Update.* http://www.vch.ca/media/VCH-anti-bullying-open-board-feb-2105.pdf
- Vieten, Cassandra; Scammell, Shelley (2015) *Spiritual & Religious Competencies In Clinical Practice. Guidelines for Psychotherapists & Mental Health Professionals.* New Harbinger Publishers Inc. Oakland, CA
- Violet Flame (2016) *The Secret Of the Violet Flame.* http://violetflame.com/violet-flame-secret/
- Virtue. D. and Lukomski, J. (2005) *Crystal Therapy. How to Heal and Empower your Life with Crystal Energy.* Hay House: CA
- Virtue, D. *Chakra Clearing. Awakening Your Spiritual Power to Know and Heal.* Hay House, Inc. 1998
- Virtue, D. (1999) *Healing With The Angels.* Hay House Inc. CA

- Virtue, D. (2008). *Angel Numbers, 101. The Meaning of 111, 123, 444, And Other Number Sequences.* Hay House.
- Wang, Christine. Symbolism of Color and Color Meanings around the Word. 15.04.2015.
www.shutterstock.com/blog/color-symbolism-and-meanings-around-the-world
- Wills, Pauline, Colour Therapy, *The Use of Colour for Health and Healing.*
- Weil, Andrew, M.D. (1995) *Spontaneous Healing.* A Ballantine Book, Ballantine Publishing Co. (p.170)
- Weil. A. *Dr. Weil's Breathing Exercises: 4-7-8: http://www.drweil.com/videos-features/videos/the-4-7-8-breath-health-benefits-demonstration/*
- White, Judith B and Langer, Ellen J: "Horizontal Hostility: Relations Between Similar Minority Groups", Journal of Social Scientists, Vol. 55, No. 3, 1999, pp. 537-559
- Wilde, Stuart. (1987) *Affirmations,* by Dove International Inc. Taos, New Mexico, USA
- Wilde, Stuart. (1988) *The Quickening.* Hay House Inc.
- Wills, Pauline, (1993) *Colour Therapy*, in Health Essentials, the use of Colour for Health and Healing
- Wright, Angela. (2008-2016) *The Colour Affect Systems.* Colour Affects. http:/.www.colour-affects.co.uk/the-colour-affects-system2008-1016

Appendix
Suggestions for Building a Self-Care Plan

Step 1: Self-Care Assessment

A self-care assessment is a non-judgmental self-assessment of personal strengths and vulnerabilities in how we structure and balance our daily activities in addition to our strategies in coping with stress.

Consider the categories of mind, body, emotion, and spirit and ask yourself:

- In what ways do I already actively support my mental, physical, emotional and spiritual needs?
- What are the areas needing more support and do I have plans to meet them?
- Do I have enough of a work/home balance?
- How do I cope with stress – positively or negatively?
- Are there short-term changes I can make to improve my self-care plan?
- What kind of assistance do I need to make other necessary changes to my self-care plan?

Self-Care Assessment Check List

Tick off the areas you already participate in then choose by highlighting other areas you want to initiate.

Physical

— Sufficient sleep
— Healthy eating
— Hydration
— Forms of short or longer timed exercise (walking, running, yoga, swim, cycling, hike, dance, tennis, etc.)
— Relaxation time-outs during the day
— Time alone during the day
— Time out in nature
— Deep breathing
— Listen to your body to find areas of stress
— Massage or other complimentary relaxation methods
— A vacation that is at a significant distance from home or overseas
— Other:

Psychological

— Reading for interest/enjoyment
— Forms of puzzles for mind exercises
— Games with self and/or others
— Personal writing (journaling)
— Deep breathing and/or meditation for mind calming
— Spend time in nature
— Short or longer term vacations
— Lighten yourself and others, with activities that promote laughter
— Attend events that are new and share ideas with different people
— Practice not analyzing situations or people
— Turn off the news
— Decide to learn something new and fun
— See where you are naturally creative and develop it further
— Know what your boundaries are and respect them
— Other:

Emotional

- Connect with people you've not seen for a while
- Spend time with positive people that support your best interests
- Look for your own strengths and accomplishments and congratulate yourself by word and deeds
- Tell *yourself* as much as you can, "I love you_____"
- Listen to good music, attend a symphony or concert you enjoy
- Attend a play
- Sing or join a choir for your own enjoyment
- Dine in a more expensive restaurant because you deserve it
- Deal with any ongoing anxieties, traumas or ongoing addictions by seeing an appropriate support counselor
- Volunteer where it is not stressful, fits your schedule, and you can make a difference
- Regulate down or turn off the news
- Other:

Spiritual

- Deep breathing and forms of meditation
- Walk in nature and breath in the life force all around you
- Spend time with animals
- Time with plants or in a garden
- Go inside your heart and ask how it feels or what it wants to do
- Read or listen to something daily that inspires you
- Repeat statements daily that affirm your strengths, your deepest wishes for how you want to see your life unfold
- Think of what you are grateful for
- Forgive and accept yourself and others as much as possible
- Practice random acts of kindness
- Spend time in a spiritual group that uplifts you
- Practice allowing things to flow (letting go of needing to control)

— Allow others to give to you
— Tell people anything you like or appreciate about them
— Appreciate the journey of courage you are on

Step 2: Daily and Weekly Planning

What routines work for others may not work for you. Implement the easiest, small-step strategies first.

- Maintain already established healthy areas
- Add in self-care practices in more vulnerable areas
- Structure in a daily and then weekly routine

Step 3: Commitment and Follow-through

- Make a commitment on a daily basis to follow-through on your plan
- Make adjustments as necessary

Step 4: Structure in Support for Commitment

- Always plan self-care routines a day ahead
- Prepare for challenges or emergency situations.
- Structure visible or technical reminders
- Share your plan with others
- Participate in similar activities with others
- Keep congratulating yourself for any positive changes you make
- Be gentle and patient
- Affirm your well-being

Index

197